Strategies to Support Struggling Adolescent Readers, Grades 6-12

Strategies to Support Struggling Adolescent Readers, Grades 6-12

Lisa Hollihan Allen
and Katherine S. McKnight

ROWMAN & LITTLEFIELD
Lanham • Boulder • New York • London

Published by Rowman & Littlefield
A wholly owned subsidiary of The Rowman & Littlefield Publishing Group, Inc.
4501 Forbes Boulevard, Suite 200, Lanham, Maryland 20706
www.rowman.com

Unit A, Whitacre Mews, 26-34 Stannary Street, London SE11 4AB

British Library Cataloguing in Publication Information Available

Library of Congress Cataloging-in-Publication Data

Names: McKnight, Katherine S. (Katherine Siewert), author. | Allen, Lisa Hollihan, author.
Title: Strategies to support struggling adolescent readers, grades 6–12 / Katherine S. McKnight and Lisa Hollihan Allen.
Description: Lanham : Rowman & Littlefield, [2018] | Includes bibliographical references and index.
Identifiers: LCCN 2018004270 (print) | LCCN 2018006427 (ebook) | ISBN 9781475822076 (Electronic) | ISBN 9781475822052 (cloth : alk. paper) | ISBN 9781475822069 (pbk. : alk. paper)
Subjects: LCSH: Reading—Remedial teaching. | Reading (Secondary)
Classification: LCC LB1050.5 (ebook) | LCC LB1050.5 .M2155 2018 (print) | DDC 372.43—dc23
LC record available at https://lccn.loc.gov/2018004270

Printed in the United States of America

Contents

Acknowledgments

First, a colossal thank you to Katie McKnight, who so generously agreed to coauthor this book with me. I am grateful we met—and hit it off—while working together on the Cooperative Educational Service Agency (CESA) 7 ELA Curriculum Companion. Our love for our students and for secondary literacy fueled us to write this book for teachers everywhere.

Thank you to the West De Pere School District, De Pere, Wisconsin, the Board of Education, and Superintendent John Zegers for recognizing and addressing the need for secondary literacy intervention in our district. Thank you to our amazing curriculum director, Amy LaPierre, for being so forward thinking and supportive as she expertly guides all of the "literacy people" in West De Pere.

Thank you to Missy Hagel, my next door teacher and fellow 6–12 literacy interventionist, for helping every time I burst into her classroom with statements like, "The Google bullets won't listen to me!" Thank you to Nicci Verbeten for all of her patient tech assistance.

Thank you to my first English teacher mentor and eventually my "teacher's principal," Irene Hucek, for listening, teaching, and encouraging. I have worked with some outstanding teachers of literacy. Our conversations, questions, and collaborations make us all better teachers. Thank you Carrie Burch, Laurie Przybylski-LaMere, Ann Barsczc, Jill Miller, Jenny Pierre, Vicki Marotz, Tara VonThoma, and Chris Seroogy.

Thank you to my students. I am so lucky I get to teach. The culture we create in our classroom as we're learning makes me love coming to school every day.

And finally, thank you to my family. My husband Scott's belief and support (and pizza from Hot Stone when I was working at our cottage) is appreciated. Thanks also to our kids—Paul and Emily—for their excitement and interest in my adventures.

Katie would like to thank her coauthor as well. Lisa's incredible classroom knowledge is a gift to all teachers. She has a keen ability to translate theory and research into practical strategies to develop the skills that teenagers need to become independent readers.

When Lisa and I first took on this project our focus was always on middle and secondary school colleagues who were frustrated that they didn't have the skills and knowledge they needed to help their students who were struggling with reading in the different disciplines. The National Assessment for Educational Progress consistently documents that the majority of our adolescent readers struggle with proficiency. Consequently, we want to thank our colleagues who gave us feedback, ideas, and encouragement along the way.

Lisa and I would also like to thank Susan Canavan, who offered us suggestions and a tremendous amount of patience. We would also like to thank Elaine Carlson and Kris Lantzy who provided support as we wordsmithed and crafted the manuscript. We are also very grateful to Richard Cash, EdD, whose expertise on self-regulation provided a much needed and appreciated addition to this book.

Introduction

"People have been trying to teach me to read since I was in kindergarten. What makes you think you can do it?" Bryce, the sullen eighth grader, said.

Bryce sat in Lisa's classroom, arms crossed defiantly, with a look of "How dare you try to teach me how to read" on his face. Bryce was in eighth grade and he had some discipline issues—issues that were directly related to his inability to read. He was frustrated and so far his experience in school had been filled with academic disappointment. Unflappable, Lisa took on the challenge. Drawing on her expertise as a reading specialist, she turned to the Wilson Reading System which systematically teaches students how to decode and encode (spell) through the structure of language, breaking it down into the most basic phonemes.

In a short period of time, Lisa and Bryce found some synergy and trust through their early success. In the subsequent weeks and months, Bryce went from mouthing and using gibberish in choir class to actually reading the lyrics. True, he probably wasn't reading all of the lyrics, but he now had the confidence to try. He was developing the skills he needed to decode textual language.

Lisa also noticed in using the approach that her high school students had similar successes. For example, Quentin, an athletic, personable sophomore, finally learned to read the text and logos on track meet signage—logos that he had previously viewed only as pictures or symbols with no textual meaning. Taylor, a student who had never felt confident in her reading ability, became an eager reader through the read aloud strategy that was a common practice in Lisa's class. Taylor transformed from a reluctant reader to one who requested books as gifts and developed greater confidence as an independent reader.

Bryce and his classmates Quentin and Taylor are students who demand our best, and as a result, make us better teachers. They are struggling and discouraged and sometimes demonstrate behavioral issues because they can't read. This book is about them—kids like Bryce, Quentin, and Taylor. *They can learn to read.* We need to provide all of the tools they need to "break the code" of textual language, even if it happens as late as middle school or high school.

When students are in elementary school, a teacher who has expertise in teaching the fundamentals of reading instructs them. At the middle and high school level that stops—and the timing could not be worse. The common belief is that as soon as students have *learned to read*, we can expect them to *read to learn*. The literacy demands increase exponentially, yet typically schools do not teach adolescents how to successfully read the increasingly difficult materials they encounter throughout their day. Literacy instruction needs to continue into middle school and high school, most especially for the students reading below grade level. For whatever reason, these students didn't develop strong literacy skills in elementary school, so now it is our responsibility to continue direct literacy (with a special focus on reading) instruction in middle and high school.

Let's be fair. For the vast majority of middle school and high school teachers, reading methodology courses were not part of our training. If we were lucky, we had a course in content reading and writing with a particular emphasis on comprehension and vocabulary. Most of us have simply not been trained to assist the students who still lack proficiency in decoding and phonics.

Both of us realized early in our careers that in order to be skilled and effective teachers, we needed a background in teaching reading and literacy. We earned graduate degrees in reading as part of our effort to tackle the adolescent reading problem. What is that problem? According to National Assessment of Educational Progress (NAEP) data cited in the Common Core State Standards (CCSS), over 60 percent of eighth and twelfth graders have not achieved grade level reading proficiency.

Of course, we do not claim to possess all of the answers to the adolescent reading problem. But we do have over fifty years of teaching experience between the two of us. We have a lot of ideas and this book is filled with them. We place a particular emphasis on decoding, vocabulary, and active reading strategies. These are the basic skills in reading, and they are the foundation for the more complex and challenging reading that students need to accomplish in middle school and high school. If students do not possess these skills, they struggle and fall further behind.

There are some basics in reading theory and research that must be understood before we discuss and contextualize strategies for your students. First we will explore current reading theory and what the National Reading Panel advises for effective instruction in reading:

The National Reading Panel's analysis made it clear that the best approach to reading instruction is one that incorporates:

- Explicit and systematic instruction in phonemic awareness
- Methods to improve fluency
- Vocabulary or discipline specific words that we need to communicate ideas and content knowledge
- Ways to enhance comprehension to convey understanding and accurate meaning

The Panel found that a combination of techniques is effective for teaching children to read:

- Phonemic awareness—the knowledge that spoken words can be broken apart into smaller segments of sound known as phonemes. Children who are read to at home—especially material that rhymes—often develop the basis of phonemic awareness. Children who are not read to will probably need to be taught that words can be broken apart into smaller sounds.
- Phonics—the knowledge that letters of the alphabet represent phonemes, and that these sounds are blended together to form written words. Readers who are skilled in phonics can sound out words they haven't seen before, without first having to memorize them.
- Fluency—the ability to recognize words easily, read with greater speed, accuracy, and expression, and to better understand what is read. Children gain fluency by practicing reading until the process becomes automatic; guided oral repeated reading is one approach to helping children become fluent readers.
- Guided oral reading—reading out loud while getting guidance and feedback from skilled readers. The combination of practice and feedback promotes reading fluency.
- Teaching vocabulary words—teaching new words, either as they appear in text, or by introducing new words separately. This type of instruction also aids reading ability.
- Reading comprehension strategies—techniques for helping individuals to understand what they read. Such techniques involve having students summarize what they've read, to gain a better understanding of the material (National Reading Panel (2000).

As stated earlier, reading education at the middle and high school level typically focuses on teaching vocabulary and building comprehension skills. The intention of this book is to provide our colleagues with lessons and materials to address the complex skills for reading achievement for those middle school and high school students who are still having difficulties with fluency and word identification.

We begin with breaking the code. The first section of the book focuses on analyzing text at the level of individual words. The majority of adolescent students will not need remediation at this level. However, we provide strategies that will support students to decode new words in a text. In the next section, we will focus on developing skills for greater comprehension through active reading strategies with a special emphasis on read alouds. Reading aloud is an effective and efficient tool to increase struggling readers' comprehension abilities. While listening to fluent reading by the teacher, the student has the opportunity to work on comprehension without the added task of decoding. They are free to visualize, predict, question, notice foreshadowing, and so on. We offer teachers tips, tricks, and a good read aloud list.

In addition to text analysis and active reading strategies, this book will explore writing lessons, activities, and strategies that enable students to express what they know and understand from their reading. Common Core State Standards require students to write clearly and coherently in the genres of argumentative, informative/explanatory, and narrative. The chapter on writing provides teachers with tools to directly teach proficient writing about reading. The range of tools begins with teaching students to scan the text for a "right there" answer, and goes all the way to having students support claims.

How will we know that the strategies are effective? Once we explore strategies for reading and writing, we offer ideas for assessment. In order to reveal how students are analyzing text, it is necessary to do a running record with each student. A running record is when the student reads a portion of text out loud to the teacher and the teacher records any errors (miscues). The teacher can then analyze the miscues and identify specific intervention points. In the last section of the book we instruct teachers how to give a running record and how to conduct a miscue analysis to guide instruction specific to each student.

As authors and teacher colleagues we have attempted to create a resource book that is based on both classroom practice and the most important research in adolescent reading.

References

National Reading Panel. (2000). Overview of report. Retrieved from https://www.nichd.nih.gov/research/supported/Pages/nrp.aspx#overview.

Part One

DECODING (THE FUNDAMENTALS OF READING)

CHAPTER 1

Breaking the Code

LETTER-SOUND RELATIONSHIP AND WORD ANALYSIS

Andrew, a seventh grade student, continuously mixes up the sounds of the digraphs /ch/ and /sh/. Sometimes he even starts reading a word that begins with /sh/ by saying "/s/ . . . Oh no! Wait! /sh/ . . . ut, shut!" and he grins good-naturedly. I always wonder just how long his good nature will last as he gets more and more behind his peers. Andrew struggles with aspects of phonemic awareness and phonics. He is at a disadvantage, but explicit instruction can help him. Most adolescents will not need extensive remediation in this area. However, because there are many who do, we'll begin by focusing on phonemic awareness, phonics, and word identification skills.

Letter-Sound Relationship

Decoding, or word identification, is the ability to decipher a particular word out of a string of letters. One of the skills necessary to decode successfully is phonemic awareness—understanding that spoken words are made up of individual units of sound—phonemes. A reader who is phonemically aware understands that the three phonemes /k/, /a/, /t/ form the word 'cat' and that the word 'shut' also has three phonemes because /sh/ is one sound. Phonetically aware readers are also able to identify and manipulate sounds. They understand that they can replace the initial sound /k/ in 'cat' with a /p/ to make a new word, 'pat.' They can replace the medial sound /a/ in 'pat' with /i/ to make 'pit.' They can replace the final sound /t/ in 'pit' with /n/ to make 'pin.'

Most students acquire this skill in kindergarten and first grade. If they did not fully develop their phonemic awareness as young children, older students can experience difficulty with decoding when they encounter unfamiliar words. This weakness becomes especially apparent as they encounter new, multisyllabic words. Shaywitz et al. asserted that students who are unsuccessful in reading words that are unfamiliar to them might also struggle with poor phonemic awareness skills (1999). This is especially problematic for adolescent readers with dyslexia. In this situation, students with significant gaps may require a systematic intervention taught with fidelity by a trained specialist. The Wilson Reading System, Lindamood-Bell LiPS, or similar programs may be appropriate for these students.

Phonics is the understanding that there is a relationship between the letters and the sounds in words. This relationship is a predictable, rule-based system for students to work within while reading and writing. Good readers can blend and segment both letters and sounds to decode unfamiliar words.

According to the National Institute for Literacy, approximately 10 percent of all adolescents struggle with word identification skills. This estimate is likely higher when we look at only struggling adolescent readers (National Institute for Literacy, 2007). Just think, if you have a hundred kids in your classroom every day, it's likely that at least ten of them are struggling with a word level deficit. Yikes—and we throw a lot of words at them! If they're missing all these words, there will also be deficits in comprehension, vocabulary, and fluency. Sometimes even if they know the word in conversation (their listening vocabulary), they are unable to decode it in print.

And it's not just about teaching students to recognize individual phonemes. As proficient readers, we don't recognize that we actually read in syllables. Struggling readers typically see the first and last letters and simply guess what the letters in between might be. In other words, they guess at the syllables and guess at the word. Consequently, readers need to recognize that the syllables are structures that create words and language. It's part of breaking the code for readers. Because it is such a big topic, we will address syllables in an upcoming chapter.

Strategies and Activities to Break the Code: Letter-Sound Relationship

Using a variety of word games, kinesthetic activities, and visual word exercises reinforces word construction, letter and sound relationships, phonics, and vocabulary development. While many of these strategies will be familiar to elementary school teachers, they all can be easily adapted with the struggling adolescent reader in mind.

TAPPING SOUNDS

Tapping Sounds is a component of the Wilson Language System and other learning to read programs. In this activity, students use their fingers to tap out different sounds. For example, for the word 'cat,' the students would finger tap for each sound with three different fingers, c-a-t. Three taps for three sounds. Since the tapping is kinesthetic, it provides an additional sensory input to simply hearing the sounds. You may believe that older students in middle school or high school would be reluctant to engage in what could be viewed as a childish practice, but once they learn the procedure you'll find that they embrace it. Maybe because it's so simple and effective students don't mind tapping to help break apart sounds in order to read and spell—in developmental reading class and in other classes, too. Eventually, tapping drops out and students are instructed to use it only when needed. It becomes a tool to use whenever they encounter an unknown word or syllable.

An example of a script for Tapping Sounds follows:

Teacher: Say, "stamp."

Student: "Stamp."

Teacher: Tap the sounds in stamp.

Student: *(Touching pointer finger to thumb)* /s/, *(middle finger to thumb)* /t/, *(ring finger to thumb)* /a/, *(pinkie finger to thumb)* /m/, *(pointer finger to thumb, again)* /p/.

Teacher: Now do it all together.

Student: *(Running thumb along tips of the fingers)* "Stamp."

MANIPULATIVES: LETTER TILES AND MAGNETIC LETTERS

 Create or purchase letter tiles or magnetic letters, using one color for consonants and digraphs and another color (preferably red) for vowels. Designating different colors helps students to distinguish between vowels and consonants. Adolescent kinesthetic learners benefit from manipulatives that help them make letter-sound connections and build words.

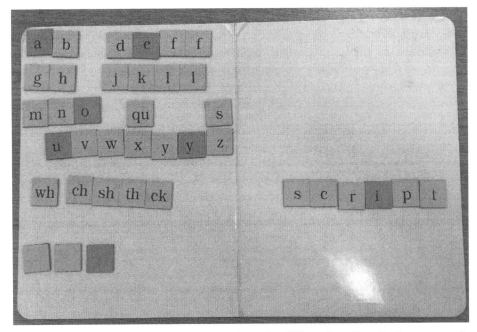

Figure 1.1.   Using letter tiles like these from the Wilson Reading System supports students of all ages as they develop their ability to make letter and sound connections. You can also make your own cut-out letter tiles out of paper.

Figure 1.2a.   Students build words with three letter blends.

Figure 1.2b.   Students work on blends on the overhead projector

HANGMAN VARIATIONS

Some old things never go out of fashion! Classic games like Hangman help students to develop greater understanding of word construction and letter-sound relationships. But you're not limited to the traditional stick figure. Older students might prefer using a picture of the school mascot or a favorite sports team cut into seven pieces. The game works the same way; it's just the picture that is different.

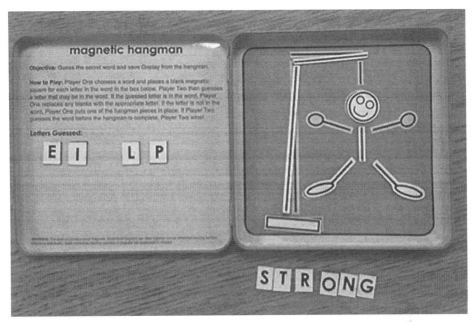

Figure 1.3. The classic Hangman game works for all ages.

Figure 1.4. A picture of the school mascot, cut into seven "puzzle pieces," makes an appealing variation for high school students.

KEYBOARDS AND TYPEWRITERS

Word construction, letter by letter, with visual and kinesthetic input is reinforced when students use computer keyboards or even old-fashioned typewriters. The demands of handwriting overwhelm some students—especially if they're also trying to concentrate on the letter-sound connection. By separating the tasks, these students are better able to focus on the relationship between sound and letter. The visual pleasure of seeing perfectly constructed letters provides valuable positive reinforcement.

Figures 1.5 and 1.6.   Typewriters and keyboards reinforce letter-by-letter word construction, with visual and kinesthetic input.

WORD LADDERS

Another exercise to reinforce word construction is Word Ladders. This word game, which according to *The Oxford Guide to Word Games* was invented by renowned author Lewis Carroll (Augarde, 2003), requires the player to fill in adjacent words that differ from each other by only one letter. In this way the player will move from the predetermined first word, to the predetermined final word. In addition to being fun, word ladders facilitate student's understanding of letter patterns that often make up words. They can be played as solitary games or, as is often more effective with older students, as a team activity. There are many sources for these puzzles, which also go by the names Laddergrams, Word-links, Word Golf, and Doublets.

An example of a simple Word Ladder follows:

Turn CAT into DOG:
    C A T
    _ _ _ (hint: a small bed)
    _ _ _ (hint: a round mark)
    D O G

WORD LADDER VARIATION: MAKING WORDS

Patricia M. Cunningham's book *Systematic Sequential Phonics They Use: For Beginning Readers of All Ages* introduces another type of word ladder she calls "Making Words" (2000, 16). In this version, students read clues and use the provided letters to form the answer word. True to its name, this book includes activities that are appealing to kindergarten students as well as older struggling readers and second-language learners.

In the example below, inspired by Cunningham's model, students are asked to use six letters to build ten words. Notice that each hint is followed by an example of the target word used in a sentence. By following the series of instructions, the word making progresses from *at* to *paint*.

Letters: a i t s p n
Words: at it pit pat spat span pan pin pain paint

1. Take two letters and make the word *at*. (Practice is at 4:00.)
2. Change one letter and make the word *it*. (*It* is important to be on time.)
3. Add one letter and make the word *pit*. (Get there early to help with the high jump *pit*.)
4. Change one letter and make the word *pat*. (The recipe in F.A.C.E. called for one *pat* of butter.)
5. Add one letter and make the word *spat*. (Usually they're best friends, but they're having a little *spat* right now.)

6. Change one letter and make the word *span*. (The Olympic swimmer Michael Phelps has an arm *span* of six feet seven inches.)
7. Take out one letter and make the word *pan*. (If you all pass the test, I will bring a *pan* of chocolate brownies.)
8. Change one letter and make the word *pin*. (Bring in a baby picture and we will *pin* them all on the wall.)
9. Add one letter and make the word *pain*. (Her injury is causing a lot of *pain*.)
10. Add one letter and make the word *paint*. (We get to *paint* today in art class.)

LISTENING WORD LADDER (A WORD LADDER VARIATION)

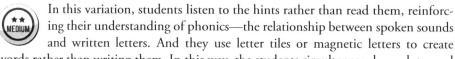 In this variation, students listen to the hints rather than read them, reinforcing their understanding of phonics—the relationship between spoken sounds and written letters. And they use letter tiles or magnetic letters to create words rather than writing them. In this way, the students simultaneously work toward speaking/listening goals while developing their fundamental reading skills. This integrated literacy is a vital component of the new standards and struggling readers are not exempt! The tactile aspect of the activity benefits kinesthetic learners.

Here's an example of a script for Listening Word Ladder.

Teacher: Use your word tiles to build the word *sun*. The sun is very warm today.
 Students use tiles to spell sun, s-u-n.
Teacher: Change one letter to make the word *fun*.
 Students remove the 's' tile and replace it with the 'f' tile, f-u-n.
Teacher: Change one letter to make the word *fan*.
 Students remove the 'u' tile and replace it with the 'a' tile, f-a-n.
Teacher: Change one letter to make *fin*. I saw the shark's fin sticking out of the water.
 Students remove the 'a' tile and replace it with the 'i' tile, f-i-n.
Teacher: Now what would you change to make the word *fish*?
 Students remove the 'n' tile and replace it with the 'sh' tile, f-i-sh.

If time permits, reinforce the concepts by repeating the activity by working backward from the concluding word to the beginning word.

WEBSITES AND APPS

  There are many apps and websites to help develop a reader's understanding of letter-sound relationship. The following list of games includes some that have been specifically developed for older students.

Bookworm

http://www.popcap.com/bookworm

Bookworm is a word-puzzle game. Players link letter tiles to build words. Bigger words earn higher scores. Burning letters add a twist to the game.

iLetterz

https://itunes.apple.com/us/app/iletterz-guess-words-by-definition/id650407138?mt=8

In iLetterz players see a description word and guess the word by filling in letters. Players complete as many words as they can to beat the clock and move on to the next level.

Letterpress

https://itunes.apple.com/us/app/letterpress-word-game/id526619424?mt=8

Letterpress is a fun puzzle game with added strategy; players can steal tiles and color the board in their favor.

SpellTower

https://itunes.apple.com/us/app/spelltower/id476500832?mt=8

SpellTower is a word game similar to Boggle. Players find words on a grid of letters, make words, and clear extra letters from the grid. Tiles rise from the bottom of the screen and players try to keep them down. If letters get to the top row, the game will be over.

Words with Friends

https://www.zynga.com/games/words-friends

Words with Friends is a game similar to Scrabble. Players are connected by Facebook or usernames. They take turns building words across the puzzle board and can chat with opponents in the app.

Word Streak with Friends

https://itunes.apple.com/us/app/scramble-with-friends-free/id485084223?mt=8

Word Streak with Friends is a fast, fun game of word finding. Words are identified in a letter board for points.

What's the Phrase?

https://itunes.apple.com/us/app/whats-the-phrase-free/id594002471?mt=8

Players choose from over forty categories and see how quickly they can guess phrases, create their own puzzles, and share with friends.

Word Search: Word Swipe

https://itunes.apple.com/us/app/word-swipe-word-search/id620072282?mt=8

Players swipe over words to form new words found in the word lists. Earn points by finding words quickly. There are four modes of play: Normal, Medium, Hard, and Expert.

Word Analysis: Breaking Down Words to Build Meaning

Seventh grader Missy was reading a section of Twilight *out loud to me because it was a part she really liked and wanted to show me. She came across the word 'unconditionally,' paused for a split second, shrugged while making a short "hhmm" sound, skipped it, and just kept on going. When she was done I asked her why she skipped that word and she said, "If I can't know it right away, I just skip it. That's what I always do."*

This isn't an isolated incident. When students come across a long word while they are reading independently, there's an excellent chance that they're just going to skip it. They don't have another strategy. Sometimes they can get away with it if it's not crucial to the meaning of the selection. But what happens if they encounter more unfamiliar, long, complex words in their content area texts? If they skip all the "hard words" it will certainly affect their comprehension in a negative way.

In the above example, the student failed to recognize that the long word 'unconditionally' is actually composed of the common root word 'condition,' which she could have easily decoded. The prefix 'un' and two suffixes 'al' and 'ly' increased the length of the word to the extent that she didn't even try to understand it. The student's long-established coping mechanism was to skip long words, so the visual length of the word was enough to prevent her from trying. Like many struggling readers, she merely saw a bunch of letters, not the chunks: root word, prefix, and suffixes.

Adolescents who read below grade level typically do not struggle at the phonetic level, but with the more complex task of word analysis. If a student cannot read 70 percent of the words on standardized lists, some weakness in word recognition or identification is suggested. Caldwell uses this approach to identify older students who need reading intervention (Caldwell and Leslie, 2009).

Furthermore, in the most recent edition of his book *What Really Matters for Struggling Readers,* Richard Allington (2012) claims that students need to accurately read 98 percent of the words on each page in order to be considered an independent reader of that text. This marks a change. His earlier studies indicated a slightly lower threshold of 95 percent. In other words, we used to think that if a student was able to read 95 percent of the words, he could be identified as an independent reader. But that's no longer good enough. This is why it's so important for readers to develop greater word recognition competency.

In order to read competently, students need to be able to recognize common words (often referred to as sight words) automatically so that most of their brain power is being used to comprehend the text, not to decode individual words. This is also true for prefixes, suffixes, and root words. As proficient readers, we don't recognize that we read in syllables. Students who are struggling readers typically see the first and last letters and simply guess what the letters in between might be. For example, a student may encounter the word *repose* but read it as *rezone* because both words begin with the same prefix, *re-*, and end with the same letter, *e*. They have difficulty breaking the word into parts and thus are unable to decode it. In other words, they guess at the word. Consequently, readers need to recognize that the syllables are structures that create words and language. It's part of breaking the code for readers.

We'll conclude this chapter by focusing on the importance of teaching words at the morphemic level in order to prepare students to tackle the reading and writing demands they will encounter across the curriculum. Morphology is the study of how words are formed. Struggling readers who are not aware of the morphological structure of words have difficulty recognizing and learning words. We will cover word families, suffixes and prefixes, root words, and sight words.

WORD FAMILY TOOLS

Word families, or phonograms or rimes, or "chunks," are words that share a pattern of letters. The "chunk" begins from the vowel and goes to the end of the word or syllable. A basic word family is –at. Words that belong in the –at word family are cat, bat, mat, pat. These are simple words, but once a student is familiar with the thirty or so most common word families, they can use them to decode five hundred single syllable words. Also, we can think about word families in syllables too. The four-syllable word 'category' contains the –at word family. When students recognize the /at/ together as one unit instead of /a/ and then /t/, the easier it will be to decode words like 'category,'

-ack pack, attack	-at bat, chat	-ide ride, decide	-ock sock, block
-all hall, install	-ate gate, debate	-ight might, delight	-oke joke, awoke
-ain rain, complain	-aw draw, straw	-ill hill, skill	-op stop, laptop
-ake cake, awake	-ay day, display	-in pin, within	-ore more, store
-ale pale, stale	-eat neat, treat	-ine fine, decline	-orn born, thorn
-ame name, game	-ell bell, shell	-ing ring, spring	-ot got, forgot
-an ran, Japan	-est best, unrest	-ink pink, sink	-ug bug, shrug
-ank bank, thank	-ice nice, price	-ip sip, chip,	-ump jump, clump
-ap cap, scrap	ick pick, click	-it sit, admit	-unk junk,chipmunk
-ash cash, splash			

Chart 1.1.   Thirty-seven common word families with example words.

'patronize,' and 'attentively.' As they gain familiarity with recognizing word families, students will be able to read higher-level words with greater fluency.

Note: The terms *word families*, *phonograms and rimes*, and *chunks* can be used interchangeably. *Word families* might seem immature for older students so it is fine to substitute one of these other terms.

When helping a student decode a word, prompt them to look for common patterns. Students highlight word families in a paragraph, a list of words, or after sorting.

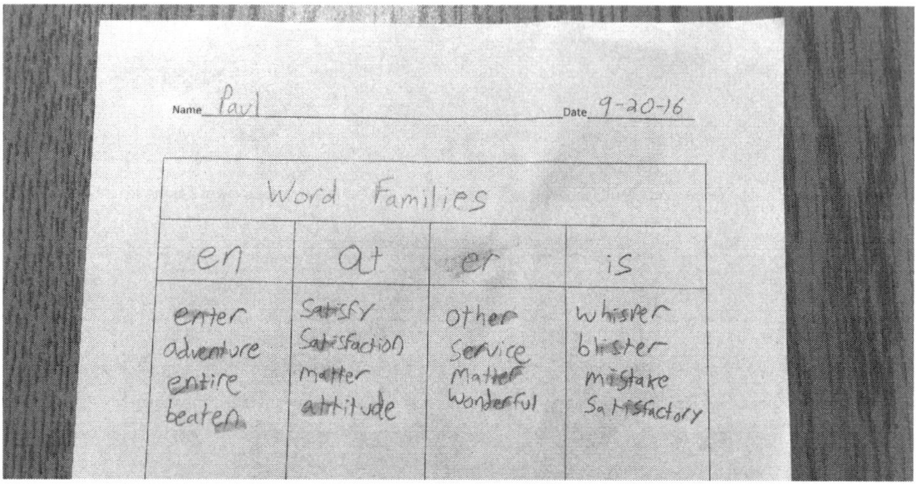

Figure 1.7. In this example, a student highlighted word families after sorting words into a graphic organizer.

Figure 1.8. Students play Scrabble with word families.

Figures 1.9 and 1.10.   Students make words with word family blocks.

SUFFIX AND PREFIX TOOL

Another word analysis tool is to look for affixes. Affixes are letter(s) added to a word to change the meaning. Prefixes are found at the beginning of a word. The most common prefix is *un-* which means not or opposite of. When you add the prefix *un-* to the word *constitutional*, you have a new word, *unconstitutional*—not or the opposite of constitutional. Suffixes are added at the end of words. The most common suffixes are *–s* and *–es*, which make words plural. The suffixes *–ous, –eous,* and *–ious* mean having the quality of. If you add *–ous* to the noun *courage*, you have a new word, the adjective *courageous*—having the quality of courage.

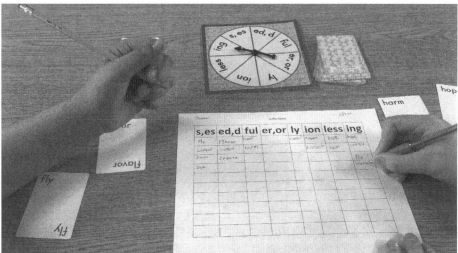

Figures 1.11–1.14. Students play games with affixes.

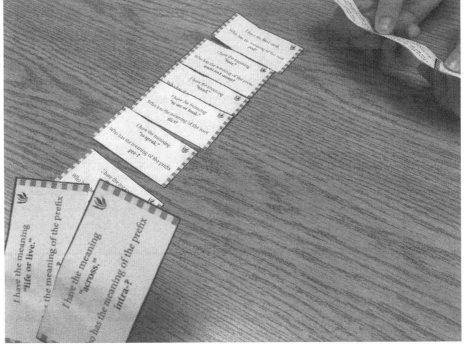

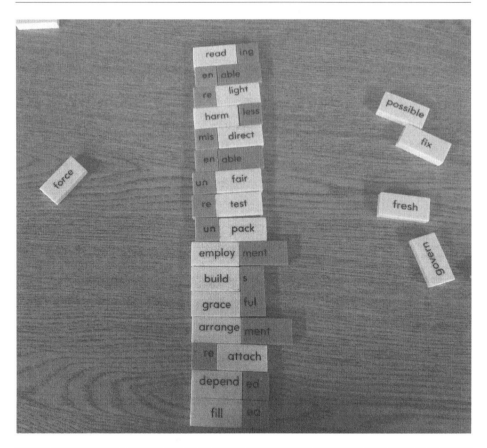

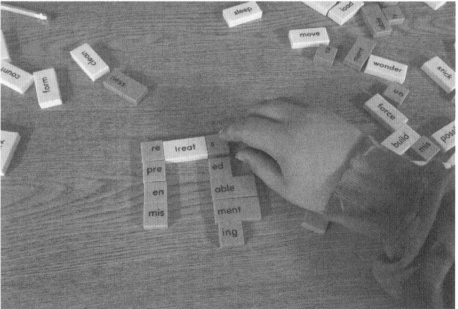

Figures 1.15 and 1.16.   Students form words with affix blocks.

ROOT WORD TOOLS

Noticing root words can help students decode words. A root is the basis of a word that holds meaning, but usually isn't a word by itself. For example the root word *sist* means to make firm, to stay, but there is no such word as *sist*—you have to add prefixes and suffixes—*insist, persisted, desist, inconsistently*, and so on. When we teach our students to recognize root words (which are short) and prefixes and suffixes (which are short and most of them are easy), a big, long, six-syllable word like *unconditionally* isn't so scary.

Common Latin Roots

Latin Root	Definition	Example
ambi	both	ambiguous, ambidextrous
aqua	water	aquarium, aquamarine
aud	to hear	audience, audition
bene	good	benefactor, benevolent
cent	one hundred	century, percent
circum	around	circumference, circumstance
contra/counter	against	contradict, encounter
dict	to say	dictation, dictator
duc/duct	to lead	conduct, induce
fac	to do; to make	factory, manufacture
form	shape	conform, reform
fort	strength	fortitude, fortress
fract	break	fracture, fraction
ject	throw	projection, rejection
jud	judge	judicial, prejudice
mal	bad	malevolent, malefactor
mater	mother	maternal, maternity
mit	to send	transmit, admit
mort	death	mortal, mortician
multi	many	multimedia, multiple
pater	father	paternal, paternity
port	to carry	portable, transportation
rupt	to break	bankrupt, disruption
scrib/script	to write	inscription, prescribe
sect/sec	to cut	bisect, section
sent	to feel; to send	consent, resent
spect	to look	inspection, spectator
struct	to build	destruction, restructure
vid/vis	to see	televise, video
voc	voice; to call	vocalize, advocate

Chart 1.2.   Common Latin Roots from *The Reading Puzzle: Word Analysis* (E. K. McEwan, 2008). Reprinted with permission of Corwin Press.

Common Greek Roots

Greek Root	Definition	Example
anthropo	man; human; humanity	anthropologist, philanthropy
auto	self	autobiography, automobile
bio	life	biology, biography
chron	time	chronological, chronic
dyna	power	dynamic, dynamite
dys	bad; hard; unlucky	dysfunctional, dyslexic
gram	thing written	epigram, telegram
graph	writing	graphic, phonograph
hetero	different	heteronym, heterogeneous
homo	same	homonym, homogenous
hydr	water	hydration, dehydrate
hyper	over; above; beyond	hyperactive, hyperbole
hypo	below; beneath	hypothermia, hypothetical
logy	study of	biology, psychology
meter/metr	measure	thermometer, perimeter
micro	small	microbe, microscope
mis/miso	hate	misanthrope, misogyny
mono	one	monologue, monotonous
morph	form; shape	morphology, morphing
nym	name	antonym, synonym
phil	love	philanthropist, philosophy
phobia	fear	claustrophobia, phobic
photo/phos	light	photograph, phosphorous
pseudo	false	pseudonym, pseudoscience
psycho	soul; spirit	psychology, psychic
scope	viewing instrument	microscope, telescope
techno	art; science; skill	technique, technological
tele	far off	television, telephone
therm	heat	thermal, thermometer

Chart 1.3.   Common Greek Roots from *The Reading Puzzle: Word Analysis* **(E. K. McEwan, 2008). Reprinted with permission of Corwin Press.**

Common Prefixes		
Prefix	**Definition**	**Example**
anti-	against	anticlimax
de-	opposite	devalue
dis-	not; opposite of	discover
en-, em-	cause to	enact, empower
fore-	before; front of	foreshadow, forearm
In-, im-	in	income, impulse
in-, im-, il-, ir-	not	indirect, immoral, illiterate, irreverent
inter-	between; among	interrupt
mid-	middle	midfield
mis-	wrongly	misspell
non-	not	nonviolent
over-	over; too much	overeat
pre-	before	preview
re-	again	rewrite
semi-	half; partly; not fully	semifinal
sub-	Under	subway
super-	above; beyond	superhuman
trans-	across	transmit
un-	not; opposite of	unusual
under-	under; too little	underestimate

Chart 1.4.   Common Prefixes from *The Reading Puzzle: Word Analysis* (E. K. McEwan, 2008). Reprinted with permission of Corwin Press.

Common Suffixes		
Suffix	**Definition**	**Example**
-able, -ible	is; can be	affordable, sensible
-al, -ial	having characteristics of	universal, facial
-ed	past tense verbs; adjectives	the dog walked, the walked dog
-en	made of	golden
-er, -or	one who; person connected with	teacher, professor
-er	more	taller
-est	the most	tallest
-ful	full of	helpful
-ic	having characteristics of	poetic
-ing	verb forms; present participles	sleeping
-ion, -tion, -ation, -ition	act; process	submission, motion, Relation, edition
-ity, -ty	state of	activity, society
-ive, -ative, -itive	adjective form of noun	active, comparative, sensitive
-less	without	hopeless
-ly	how something is	lovely
-ment	state of being; act of	contentment
-ness	state of; condition of	openness
-ous, -eous, -ious	having qualities of	riotous, courageous, gracious
-s, -es	more than one	trains, trenches
-y	characterized by	gloomy

Chart 1.5.   Common Suffixes from *The Reading Puzzle: Word Analysis* (E. K. McEwan, 2008). Reprinted with permission of Corwin Press.

Root Words

Name/Date: _____

Root words are found in many English words.
They may seem like nonsense words, but they are not.
These roots have meaning and are used to make longer words.

Using the root word, add prefixes and/or suffixes to make new words.

chron-time	graph-writing
hypo-below, beneath	logy-study of

Root Words

Name/Date: _____

Root words are found in many English words.
They may seem like nonsense words, but they are not.
These roots have meaning and are used to make longer words.

Using the root word, add prefixes and/or suffixes to make new words.

spec-see, look	junct-join
cred-believe	sist-to make firm, to stay

Charts 1.6a–d.   Sample activities that give students opportunities to practice making words using roots, prefixes, and suffixes.

Root Words

Name/Date: _____

Root words are found in many English words.
They may seem like nonsense words, but they are not.
These roots have meaning and are used to make longer words.

Using the root word, add prefixes and/or suffixes to make new words.

aud-to hear	ject-throw
jud-judge	port-to carry

Root Words

Name/Date: _____

Root words are found in many English words.
They may seem like nonsense words, but they are not.
These roots have meaning and are used to make longer words.

Using the root word, add prefixes and/or suffixes to make new words.

photo/phos-light	tele-far off
therm-heat	dys-bad, hard, unlucky

Charts 1.6a–d. (continued) Sample activities that give students opportunities to practice making words using roots, prefixes, and suffixes.

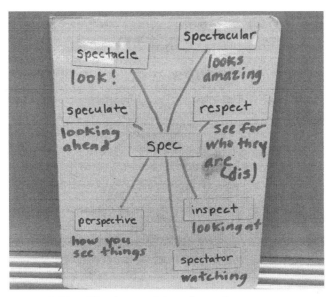

Figure 1.17. Word map for root word *spec*.

SIGHT WORDS TOOLS

It is critical that readers have the ability to access sight words or high frequency words (we will use these terms interchangeably) automatically. In other words, they have to read with some *automaticity*. If readers have to slow down to decode the word 'unconditionally' every time they come across it, they will lose the level of engagement with the meaning of the text required for quality comprehension. This is especially important when you consider that many high frequency words don't follow the rules phonetically. Think about the words *would* (why isn't it *wud*?), *because* (why isn't it *becuz*?), and *thought* (why isn't it *thot*?). Our students need to be able to recognize these words "by sight."

Figure 1.18. Students time each other as they read stacks of sight word flash-cards.

Figures 1.19 and 1.20.   Loose-leaf rings turn cards into handy personal diction-aries so students can keep challenging words accessible for both reference and practice.

Figure 1.21.   Students play Sight Word Bingo.

Figure 1.22.   Sight Word Memory is a popular game and is easily adapted for students of varying ages and abilities.

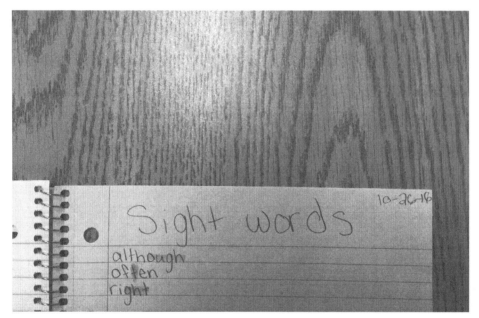

Figure 1.23. This three-step activity requires students to (1) write the challenging sight word, (2) highlight the tricky part, and (3) think of a way to remember the correct spelling. For example, "There is *often* a group *of ten*."

Figure 1.24. Practice reading and writing the words in different mediums—using white boards, gel boards, colored pencils, chalk, colored paper, typewriter, overhead, magnetic letters, items cut from magazines, and so on.

Conclusion

Most students master phonemic awareness as young children. They master lists of sight words, prefixes, suffixes, and word families. They learn to confidently disassemble unfamiliar words, look for clues in the pieces, and figure out word meanings. But for those students who miss out on that short window of opportunity, there is often no going back. Because they lack the fundamentals, they develop various predictable coping devices. They skip words or they attempt to identify words based only on first and last letters. And as they confront ever more complex texts across the curriculum, they fall further and further behind their peers. Many of them quit trying. But it doesn't have to be that way. With appropriate and timely intervention, these students can master fundamental reading skills at any age. The strategies discussed in this chapter are very similar to the strategies used with younger children—they have to be since the educational goals are the same! But with minor adaptations that are respectful of adolescent sensibilities, they can be used to prepare even the most frustrated reader for eventual college or career.

References

Allington, R. L. (2012). *What really matters for struggling readers: Designing research-based programs* (3rd ed.). Boston: Allyn and Bacon.

Augarde, T. (2003). *The Oxford guide to word games.* Oxford: Oxford University Press.

Caldwell, J., and Leslie, L. (2009). *Intervention strategies to follow informal reading inventory assessment: So what do I do now?* Boston: Pearson/Allyn and Bacon.

Cunningham, P. M. (2000). *Systematic sequential phonics they use: For beginning readers of any age.* Greensboro, NC: Carson-Dellosa.

Lindamood-Bell. (n.d.). Lindamood Phoneme Sequencing® Program for Reading, Spelling, and Speech (LiPS®). Retrieved March 11, 2016, from http://lindamoodbell.com/program/lindamood-phoneme-sequencing-program.

McEwan, E. K. (2008). *The reading puzzle: Word analysis.* Thousand Oaks, CA: Corwin Press.

Meyer, S. (2005). *Twilight Saga.* Book 1: Twilight. New York: Little, Brown Books for Young Readers, chap. 9.

National Institute for Literacy. (2007). Key literacy component: Decoding. Adapted from, What content-area teachers should know about adolescent literacy. AdLit.org. Retrieved March 10, 2016, from http://www.adlit.org/article/27875/.

Shaywitz, S. E. (2003). *Overcoming dyslexia: A new and complete science-based program for reading problems at any level.* New York: A.A. Knopf.

Shaywitz, S. E., Fletcher, J. M., Holahan, J. M., Schneider, A. E., Marchione, K. E., Stuebing, K. K., et al. (1999). Persistence of dyslexia: The Connecticut Longitudinal Study at adolescence. *Pediatrics, 104* (6).

Wilson Reading System. (n.d.). Retrieved March 10, 2016, from http://www.wilsonlanguage.com/programs/wilson-reading-system/.

Wylie, R. E., and Durrell, D. D. (1970), Teaching vowels through phonograms. Elementary English, 47, 787–91.

CHAPTER 2

Syllable Types
THE CLOVER MODEL

Sometimes the smallest things make a huge difference to a struggling reader. At this level for intervention, it's not unusual to have the same students for more than one year because it takes longer to close the gap for older students. At the beginning of one school year I overheard one of my continuing students comment to his neighbor, who was hesitating on a word, "Remember that every syllable has a vowel and then look at it that way—that's what helps me." I was stunned. I had told him that the year before, almost in passing. I remember it clearly because it seemed so self-evident and I had just assumed it was obvious to him, too. But it wasn't. Who would have thought that directly stating this one tip was going to be a game changer? It ended up being the key to helping this older, struggling reader grasp the concept of syllables. He remembered it through summer break and was able to articulate it to a peer months later! This event reminded me that good readers have internalized hundreds of reading tricks. It can sometimes surprise us, as teachers, to discover that our struggling middle and high school readers haven't picked up on them despite our best efforts. It reminded me to never assume that something is obvious just because I do it instinctively myself.

"Secondary students encounter 10,000 or more new words per year in their content area texts"—most are multisyllable (Hougen, 2014). Struggling students need a strategy for breaking long words into manageable parts to read. Many students (as well as their teachers!) have internalized the use of the six syllable types and the vowel sounds. There are students who would benefit from explicit instruction regarding the six syllable types and the vowel sounds. When they see the word 'accomplishment,' they might just see a long string of letters and just guess or go ahead and skip it. Lisa had a student who could shoot out four or five long words that started with the same letter as the word he was trying to decode. His first word analysis strategy was rapid-fire guessing—and he knew a lot of big words; he just couldn't read them. If we can prompt students by saying, "All the syllables are closed," they can then start at the beginning of the word and read across it, knowing all the vowels will be short.

Throughout this chapter you'll find written references to spoken words. I'll be using a common "code" to indicate what you would be hearing or saying if we were sitting together in the same room. Here's how that code works.

Spoken language is composed of individual sounds. We use slashes to separate the sounds when writing them out. It's important to remember that a letter between slashes represents one sound, and those are not necessarily the letters that would be used to spell that sound. Many words include a different number of letters than sounds. For example:

/b/ /oy/ = the word 'boy' and is spelled with three letters but includes two sounds; /g/ /ā/ /m/= the word 'game' is spelled with four letters but includes three sounds.

When we want to imply that *any* consonant would work—if we're discussing rhyming words for example—we use /'-'/ to indicate the missing consonant sound.

/'-'/ /a/ /t/ = could be the word fat, hat, that, mat, chat, and so on.

The Six Syllable Types

Fifty percent of all syllables are closed, so it's smart to begin with those. Closed syllables have one vowel that is followed by or "closed off" by one or more consonants making the vowel short. The word 'cat' is a closed syllable—the *a* is the only vowel and it is closed off by one or more consonants, so the vowel is short /c/ /ă/ /t/. In the word 'publish,' there are two syllables and they are both closed because they both contain one vowel that is closed off by one or more consonants pŭb lĭsh. The word 'admit' also contains two closed syllables ăd mĭt. It doesn't matter that there isn't anything before the vowel *a*: what matters in closed syllables is what comes after. Even though 'accomplishment' is a long word, if students recognize that all the syllables are closed, they can decode it ăc cŏm plĭsh mĕnt. For a struggling reader, having an effective word analysis strategy for a word with fourteen letters is quite an accomplishment!

The next syllable type is the vowel-consonant-e (v-e) syllable. You may remember it as the "silent e" or the "magic e." In a v-e syllable, the "silent/magic e" jumps over the consonant and makes the vowel say its name (a long vowel sound). You know the word 'hop' is a closed syllable /h/ /ŏ/ /p/. If we add the silent/magic e, it becomes a v-e syllable with a long vowel sound /h/ /ō/ /p/.

A third syllable type is the open syllable. The last letter in an open syllable is the vowel—it is "open to the world," it "says its name," it is the long vowel sound. The word 'go' is an open syllable. The last letter is the vowel *o*, it is open to the world, it says its name—it is the long vowel sound /g/ /ō/. (If we put a *t* at the end, it becomes a closed syllable and the vowel is now short /g/ /ŏ/ /t/.) The word 'migrate' has an open syllable and a v-e syllable mī grāte. The word 'irate' also has an open syllable and a v-e syllable ī rāte. It doesn't matter that there isn't anything before the *i*, it only matters that there is nothing after it—it's open.

The fourth syllable type is the consonant-l-e syllable (-le). In a -le syllable, the *e* is silent again. We only hear two sounds—the consonant and the *l*—the job of the *e* is to silently be the vowel in the syllable because every syllable needs a vowel. The word 'fable' has an open syllable and a -le syllable fā bl. If we were unfamiliar with the word 'fable,' but we knew about -le syllables, we'd know the first syllable wasn't pronounced /f/ /ă/ /b/ because we'd know that the -le syllable must have a consonant, an *l*, and an *e* leaving the *a* open and long. The -le syllable is always the last syllable in a word and that helps struggling readers spot them. Even longer or less common words like 'unarguable,' 'Constantinople,' and 'indelible' become more reader-friendly if a student begins by focusing on the final -le syllable.

The fifth syllable type is the r-controlled. We tell our students that the *r* messes with the vowels. The *r* has a lot of power and it can make a vowel sound change. The sound isn't long or short—it's just different. When *r* is controlling *a* it says /ar/ as in 'car.' When *r* is controlling *o* it says /or/ as in 'or.' When *r* controls *e*, *i*, and *u* it makes the same sound—it's just spelled differently—/er/ as in 'per,' /ir/ as in 'bird,' and /ur/ as in 'hurt' ('or' and 'ar' can also say /er/ as in 'doctor' and 'hangar,' but that is less common). Content area teachers will have no trouble finding vocabulary words that include this syllable type.

Science vocabulary:
    sedimen*tary*
    molecu*lar*
    in*ver*tebrate
    *per*colation
    *cir*culatory
    res*pir*ation
    au*ror*a
    ca*lor*imitry
    *sur*gical
    aper*ture*

Social Studies vocabulary:
    oli*gar*chy
    *Spar*tan
    confed*er*ation
    gov*ern*ment
    *dir*igible
    *Mir*anda Rule
    *for*ensic
    terri*tory*
    *cur*rency
    *ur*banity

The final syllable type is the double vowel. These can be tricky because there are so many combinations and sounds, but if students feel confident about the rest of the syllable types, they usually can decode these without too much difficulty.

Double vowels that have the long *a* /ā/ sound are /ai/ rain, /ay/ day (*y* acting as a vowel). Double vowels that have the long *e* /ē/ sound are /ee/ beet, /ea/ each; /ay/ or /ai/ are pronounced as a long *a* /ā/ sound—for example: claim or play; and /ea/, /ee/, or /ey/ are pronounced as a long *e* /ē/ sound—for example: neat, sleep, or valley.

The 6 Syllable Types

(listed in order of commonality in the English language)

Closed

This syllable is a vowel closed in by a consonant to make the vowel short.
Ex.   cŭp   rŏck   swĭft

Open

This syllable is a vowel at the end of a syllable to make the vowel long.
Ex.   shē   whȳ   ēven   hālō   stipūlate   hȳdrōplane

v-**E**   (vowel, consonant, e)

This syllable is a vowel, followed by a consonate, followed by an e. The final e makes the first vowel long.
Ex.   chōke   grāpevīne   compēte

-c**L**e   (consonant, le)

This syllable is a consonant, followed by -le.
Ex.   dŭffle   crādle   ămble   māple

R controlled

This syllable's vowel is controlled by the r. The vowel is not long, nor short.
Ex.   garnish   insert   thirty   organize   swerve

Double **V**owel

This syllable has 2 letters (usually vowels) working as a team to make a sound.
(ai, ay, ee, ea, ey, oi ,oy, oa, oe, ow, ou, oo, ue, ew, au, aw)

Ex.   trait   poach   drowsy   couch

Figure 2.1.   The Six Syllable Types

There are rules students can learn to break words into syllables. If students internalize these rules (like we have) they can use them to "read across the word syllable by syllable."

BREAKING WORDS INTO SYLLABLES

First, find the vowels in the word and separate them if they are not touching another vowel. Each vowel will be in its own syllable. Then, look at the letters between these vowels.

Rule #1: If there are 2 consonants, they get split. Ex. pub lish sub mit	Rule #2: The first syllable *wants* to be closed (meaning it will have a short vowel). Ex. hab it mim ic
Rule #3: Digraphs cannot be broken. (Digraphs are 2 letters that make one sound: wh,ch,sh,th ck, ph) Ex. lock et graph ic	Rule #4: If there are 3 consonants, the digraphs stay together. Ex. ath lete eth nic
Rule #5: If there are 3 consonants, the blend *usually* goes with the second syllable. Ex. ab stract con tract	Rule #6: If there are 4 consonants together, the blend will be split between them. (This keeps the digraphs, blends, and welded sounds together. These are usually compound words.) Ex. post script grand child

Chart 2.1.   Six rules for dividing syllables. Chart courtesy of Melissa Hagel.

CLOVER

The CLOVER acronym—Closed, -Le, O, double Vowel, v-E, R-controlled—is used in some elementary schools to remind readers about the six syllable types. The clover image and the acronym combine to help readers identify syllable types. Older students would benefit from the reminder too. If we use the syllable types when we introduce vocabulary, we would be giving our students another strategy to use for engaging with long words. Lisa worked with a colleague, business teacher Stephanie Reinerio, to create the following visual reference for older readers.

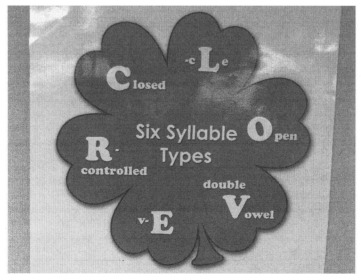

Figure 2.2.   A variation of the CLOVER model. © Lisa Hollihan Allen and Stephanie Reinerio. Reprinted with permission.

Strategies and Activities: Practicing Syllable Types

There are a wide variety of word games, kinesthetic activities, and visual word exercises that will reinforce syllable recognition. Many more can be found online or by teaming up with colleagues in the elementary grades. With a little imagination and creativity, they can be adapted for adolescent students. As with all activities, the teacher's experience is the best way to determine which activity will be most useful for each student and each situation.

MANIPULATIVES: LETTER TILES AND MAGNETIC LETTERS

Create or purchase letter tiles or magnetic letters, using one color for consonants and digraphs and another color (preferably red) for vowels. Designating different colors helps students to distinguish between vowels and consonants. Dictate words for them to build/spell. Then have them divide by syllables. Adolescent kinesthetic learners benefit from manipulatives that help them make letter-sound connections, build words, and divide words into syllables.

Figures 2.3–2.6.   A wide variety of letter tiles are suitable for classroom use.

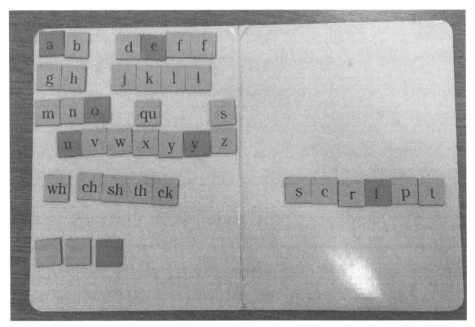

Figures 2.3–2.6.   A wide variety of letter tiles are suitable for classroom use.

SYLLABLE SCOOPING—PAPER/PENCIL VERSION

Write a list of multisyllabic words. These can be words that the class has already discussed, vocabulary words, or words that are going to be encountered in upcoming texts. Have students work independently, or with a partner to determine how many syllables are in the word.

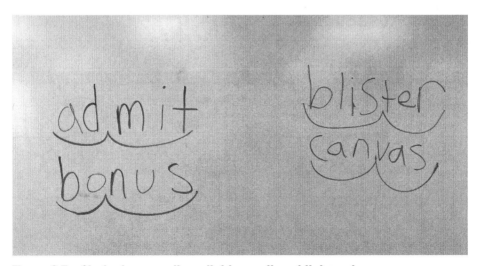

Figure 2.7.   Students scoop the syllables on the whiteboard.

Figure 2.8.   Students scoop syllables using the overhead projector.

Figure 2.9.   Students scoop syllables using syllable cards from the Wilson Language System.

Figure 2.10.   After dividing by number of syllables as a group, students work from a list to independently divide by syllables.

As a final step, have them code each syllable by type by making a predetermined symbol above each syllable. For example, you can use a dot for a closed syllable, a dash for a vowel-consonant-e syllable, a small circle for an open syllable, an L for a consonant-l-e syllable, and an R for an r-controlled syllable.

There is also an accepted coding system that makes a scoop (breve) over short vowels and a straight line (macron) over long vowels.

SYLLABLE SCOOP—MOUTH/HAND VERSION

 to This is an alternative to the Syllable Scoop—Paper/Pencil version activity. It's more likely to appeal to kinesthetic learners or be useful when working with students who are challenged by small motor activities like writing. Prepare the list of multisyllabic words as above, using vocabulary words or words that are going to be encountered in an upcoming text. Have students work independently or in pairs, making a scooping motion with their hand as they pronounce each syllable.

After each word has been scooped, the student (or their partner) should identify each type of syllable. Encourage students to refer back to the written word when they identify the syllable type. Explain that the "hints" to syllable type identification are found in the way the syllable is *spelled* as well as how it is *pronounced*. If students are working in pairs, instruct them to take turns being the scooper and the identifier.

SYLLABLE PUZZLES

 to Have students cut up printed words into syllables. They can store their paper syllables in bags or envelopes. Then students can reassemble the words by putting them together to form the original words. This activity can be used as an ongoing project, giving students a chance to revisit syllable types and reinforce their learning. New words and longer words can be added to each student's repertoire as their confidence and skills grow. Do the activity with vocabulary words, high frequency words, or use the resource lists at the end of this chapter.

Figures 2.11 and 2.12.   Students do the Syllable Puzzles using syllable cards from the Wilson Language System

GET CREATIVE!

You don't need dedicated materials in order for students to practice breaking polysyllabic words into syllables. In this example, you'll see that a teacher used leftover magnetic sheets after punching out magnetic flash cards that came with her Fountas and Pinnell's Leveled Literacy Intervention (LLI) program. Students practiced dividing words into syllables in the frames.

e	lec	tro	mag	net	ic
ex	per	i	men	ta	tion
na	no	tech	nol	o	gy
an	ti	bac	ter	i	al

Figure 2.13.

 **to** Any teacher can make a visually appealing word cloud of the elements of word recognition using an online app like Tagzedo. These word clouds are valuable as posters or reference sheets, but they have more appeal for visual learners.

Don't let lack of materials slow you down. Students can easily create their own letter set for classroom or home use. Use the template in figure 2.17 as a guide.

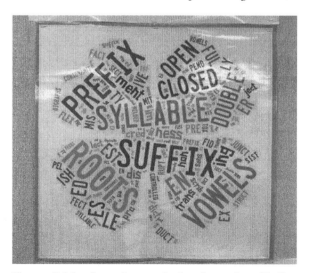

Figure 2.14. Sample word cloud made with the elements of word recognition.

a	b	c	d
e	f	g	h
i	j	k	l
m	n	o	p
qu	r	s	t
u	v	w	x
y	z		

Figure 2.15. Photocopy these letters to create your own letter sets.

Word Sorting Resources

Print out lists of words and cut them apart, then ask students to sort words by syllable type. Beginners can sort one-syllable words. Then, as they get more adept they can sort longer words by the final syllable type. Advanced learners can sort multisyllable words by the middle syllable. Use vocabulary words, high frequency words, or these word lists on the pages that follow.

One Syllable Word Sort	shop	form	world	move
shout	while	leave	force	sound
fault	weight	tide	stocks	blend
draft	tone	graph	tempt	graph
tense	quite	reign	moat	trait
seize	poise	sear	script	waive
down	stealth	sphere	prim	slight
loathe	sound	maze	norm	sound
phase	scribe	lax	whine	coin
thought	rhyme	loot	oust	know
cull	bide	through	plea	pact
bleak	vogue	sense	clan	scope
tack	shock	dull	path	state
star	eight	flight	brief	peace
serve	type	film	ride	twist

Chart 2.2. One-Syllable Word Sort

Two Syllable Word Sort	array	averse	badger	begrudge
constant	matrix	nuance	epic	surplus
language	describe	amount	statement	increase
confide	blatant	agile	suppress	comply
context	segment	neutral	create	precise
commute	attest	despite	dissent	exchange
system	recede	people	deter	dormant
follow	village	deceive	purpose	evade
finite	imply	region	function	soldier
products	ponder	angle	flagrant	famish
immune	sequence	mimic	frugal	around
compound	captain	propel	machine	network
sentence	obstruct	because	accept	recruit
subtle	novice	complete	console	culprit
drastic	paper	poison	boycott	career

Chart 2.3.   Two-Syllable Word Sort

Three Syllable Word Sort	adjacent	principle	radical	amazing
compromise	parallel	kinetic	attribute	transition
atmosphere	embargo	composite	cultural	continent
Celsius	ancestor	expression	another	substances
density	potential	devious	continued	compromise
frequency	judicial	various	property	labyrinth
relevant	agitate	example	amplitude	summarize
pacify	competent	century	primary	alternate
important	molecules	numeral	intercept	defiant
different	inversion	notation	decimal	improvise
forgery	annotate	qualify	scientist	inflection
buoyancy	government	factories	consumer	idolize
modify	credible	demolish	generate	natural
actual	financial	cultural	spatula	adventure
alignment	museum	companion	pioneer	podium

Chart 2.4. Three-Syllable Word Sort

Four Syllable Word Sort	calisthenics	optimism	coordinate	usually
participate	collaborate	preferable	consecutive	euphemism
executive	intersection	diplomacy	discriminate	criticism
citizenship	composition	appropriate	eliminate	continental
independent	variable	spontaneous	prerequisite	particular
capacity	alternative	sympathetic	irrational	adversity
renewable	illuminate	inadequate	velocity	combination
hypothesis	propaganda	diagonal	secondary	exponential
temperature	universal	hypocrisy	coincidence	transformation
corresponding	mandatory	combination	revolution	integration
imitation	belligerent	inaudible	inefficient	arbitrary
atrocity	auxiliary	negotiate	geology	evacuate
geometric	reorganize	reasonable	geranium	enjoyable
plentiful	sympathetic	identical	preposition	ordinary
celebration	relaxation	alligator	invisible	relationship

Chart 2.5.   Four-Syllable Word Sort

Five Syllable Word Sort	nonrenewable	preoccupation	superintendent	administrator
determination	ceremonial	abbreviation	probability	nationality
animosity	insignificant	procrastination	interdependence	equilateral
capitalism	supplementary	psychological	photosynthesis	characteristic
inequality	probability	justification	similarity	opportunity
vaporization	approximation	communication	representative	nationalism
experimental	complementary	reactionary	actuality	opportunity
claustrophobia	alliteration	unidentified	personality	justifiable
anniversary	electricity	multiplication	appreciation	individual
generosity	insignificant	evaporation	representative	abbreviation
characteristics	imaginary	refrigerator	cafeteria	undeniable
orientation	anticipation	elimination	vocabulary	international
hypothermia	inspirational	accommodation	figuratively	sociology
absentmindedness	archaeology	auditorium	equilateral	overachiever
irresponsible	sensitivity	clarification	notification	probability

Chart 2.6.   Five-Syllable Word Sort

Six Syllable Word Sort	idiosyncrasy	unsophisticated	biodiversity	archaeological
organizational	electromagnetic	geopolitical	onomatopoeia	chronologically
generalization	anthropomorphism	capitalization	responsibility	overpopulation
personification	extraterrestrial	veterinarian	encyclopedia	characterization
revolutionary	identification	humanitarian	autobiography	demobilization
adaptability	identifiable	dependability	cardiovascular	acetaminophen
discombobulated	acceptability	involuntarily	invisibility	disobedience
rehabilitation	responsibilities	insubordination	divisibility	internalization
misrepresentation	applicability	unimaginable	popularization	nanotechnology
nonparticipation	reliability	fundamentalism	rationalization	colonialism
admissibility	capitalization	commercialization	cinematography	deniability
experimentation	overcompensation	onomatopoetic	nationalization	vulnerability
environmentalist	availability	eventuality	marginalization	antibacterial
misinterpretation	disorganization	unconditionally	valedictorian	advisability
performability	visualization	unabbreviated	accessibility	mispronunciation

Chart 2.7. Six-Syllable Word Sort

Mixed Syllable Word Sort	family	rich	intelligence	forgiveness
authority	revolution	complicated	discrimination	globalization
education	trigonometry	calendar	once	evaporation
hospital	computer	happiness	necessary	overpopulation
advertising	professional	territory	anniversary	example
amazing	green	seventeen	gate	strength
ice	mystery	inspiration	syllable	identifiable
pediatrician	imagination	insignificant	extraterrestrial	pandemonium
exterminate	equality	technology	be	encyclopedia
ordinary	memories	politics	helicopter	victory
positive	world	perimeter	parallelogram	humanitarian
acceleration	identical	intimidating	secretary	generalization
government	musical	library	elementary	subtraction
adorable	perfection	life	radio	autobiography
confidence	overcompensation	innocent	appreciation	microbiology

Chart 2.8. Mixed-Syllable Word Sort

Syllable Puzzle Resources

Have students cut up printed words into syllables. They can store their paper syllables in bags or envelopes. Then students can reassemble the words by putting them together to form the original words.

Syllable Puzzle examples.

Words by Syllable All Closed	pub	lish	in	dent
him	self	bet	ter	prob
lem	hun	dred	sud	den
pres	ent	ex	press	ex
pect	mag	net	ac	quire
ob	ject	can	not	hap
pen	up	on	ob	ject
sud	den	sub	ject	sum
mer	writ	ten	pres	ent
Fin	ish	them	selves	with
in	stat	us	blem	ish
dis	rupt	en	list	ex
cel	in	vent	ab	sent
plan	et	con	flict	in
dex	con	trast	den	tist

Chart 2.9.   Closed Syllable Puzzle Words

Words by Syllable	be	gin	in	clude
Closed and Open	bro	ken	mo	ment
stu	dents	hu	man	si
lent	re	flect	rep	tile
pro	ton	re	tell	pre
fix	re	port	the	sis
ma	trix	pro	pel	di
vert	e	mit	flu	ent
i	con	ma	trix	mot
to	no	mad	pol	lute
qui	et	re	lent	re
pel	tri	dent	si	nus
re	spect	re	set	re
strict	va	cant	de	flect

Chart 2.10.   Closed and Open Syllable Puzzle Words

Words by Syllable	com	plete	de	cide
Closed and v-e	care	ful	in	side
State	ment	en	tire	vol
ume	in	come	dec	ade
ex	treme	do	nate	en
grave	ex	clude	im	mune
in	trude	mis	place	name
less	neg	ate	tell	tale
trans	late	un	wise	vol
ume	con	fuse	um	pire
ath	lete	up	grade	en
tire	con	crete	hand	shake
ad	mire	frus	trate	base
ment	es	cape	pan	cake

Chart 2.11.   Closed and v-E Syllable Puzzle Words

Words by Syllable	num	ber	o	ver
Mixed and r-controlled	dif	fer	ev	er
per	son	sur	face	per
haps	cen	ter	farm	ers
for	est	win	ter	won
der	sur	prise	lev	er
riv	er	des	ert	rur
al	ur	ban	ex	port
im	port	chap	ter	ad
verb	gar	nish	in	vert
la	ter	lev	er	mi
ser	nar	rate	net	work
plat	ter	skirm	ish	so
lar	lu	nar	gar	den

Chart 2.12.   Mixed R-controlled Syllable Puzzle Words

Words by Syllable	mid	dle	peo	ple
Mixed and -le	man	tle	fa	ble
cir	cle	ta	ble	sam
ple	nee	dle	ma	ple
twin	kle	wrin	kle	bea
gle	no	ble	bun	dle
pur	ple	tum	ble	ap
ple	puz	zle	can	dle
baf	fle	bri	dle	dwin
dle	kin	dle	scut	tle
gam	ble	grap	ple	guz
zle	jug	gle	scrib	ble
shuf	fle	hum	ble	fum
ble	strug	gle	ca	ble

Chart 2.13.   Mixed -Le Syllable Puzzle Words

Words by Syllable	a	round	ex	plain
Mixed and Double Vowel	with	out	rea	son
out	side	in	stead	leaf
let	main	tain	mea	ger
mis	count	noise	less	out
break	out	rage	pau	per
peace	ful	per	form	re
claim	year	ling	stee	ple
in	deed	rail	road	char
coal	val	ue	re	joice
res	cue	auth	or	tur
moil	loi	ter	top	soil
thou	sand	dis	count	dream
er	cou	pon	car	toon

Chart 2.14.   Mixed Double Vowel Syllable Puzzle Words

Words by Syllable	become	produce	beside	remain
All Mixed	contain	teacher	garden	corner
provide	repeat	detail	locate	wavelength
protein	leader	season	market	repeal
crusade	empire	decode	belief	timeline
cosine	ego	exceed	debate	expect
famish	fickle	finite	frantic	glimmer
gusto	havoc	irate	ladle	metric
migrate	mimic	minion	mishap	nestle
nimble	obstruct	persist	ponder	prefer
precise	profile	rapid	reform	retrace
savor	treble	valid	vendor	veto
revise	rotate	yoga	refund	impulse
promote	instruct	argue	torment	concern

Chart 2.15.   Mixed Syllable Puzzle Words

Conclusion

When Katie works in schools, middle school and high school teachers will often express their concern that students may be reading at a 200 or 300 Lexile level. When Katie exclaims, "That's *awesome*. We don't have to go back to the decoding or syllabic level!" the teachers look at her like she's nuts. Once students "crack the code," they become better readers with greater experience. Meaning, the more students read, the better they become at vocabulary and comprehension. If students do not "crack the code" by the time they enter middle school and high school, we have to directly teach about decoding. Now that we have offered some activities and strategies for decoding that can remediate these issues for students, the next chapter will explore vocabulary.

References

Hougen, M. *Evidence-Based Reading Instruction for Adolescents, Grades 6–12* (Document No. IC-13). Retrieved from University of Florida, Collaboration for Effective Educator, Development, Accountability, and Reform Center Website: http://ceedar.education.ufl.edu/tools/innovation-configurations/.

CHAPTER 3

Vocabulary

WHY WORDS MATTER FOR LEARNING AND READING

Whenever middle school and high school teachers, assembled for professional development, are asked, What is the most challenging part of presenting discipline-specific texts to students? they overwhelmingly respond, "vocabulary!" When they're prompted to reflect on that answer, the teachers go on to explain that introducing new vocabulary to adolescent learners who are still struggling with reading basics is particularly frustrating. Like all of us, they recognize that competent readers determine and clarify word meanings while they read. They know that competent writers choose appropriate words and phrases so they can express what they've learned. The frustration arises because these teachers don't know how to help students develop those skills and relate them to their specific content. In this chapter, we will provide strategies to support all students, but particularly struggling readers, as they learn to understand new words wherever they encounter them.

In order to be college and career ready, students must have developed vocabulary skills in which there is advanced understanding of figurative language, word relationships, and nuances of meaning. Students also need to develop their understanding and knowledge of academic and domain-specific language that they may need for either college or career. Most importantly, our students need to know how to choose appropriate words and phrases on their own so that they can express what they know and understand.

In the past, students would frequently memorize long lists of words that were given to them by their teachers. They were encouraged to learn vocabulary words through skill and drill activities. We know that this is *not* the most effective approach.

The most *effective* way to develop vocabulary in students is through exposure to new vocabulary with increased amounts of reading and "playing" with words. Students also benefit from the consideration of the qualities and relationships between words. They also benefit from the examination of word structures, root words, and influences from other languages.

What the Experts Say about Vocabulary Development

There has been much research and discussion about vocabulary development. Robert Marzano (2004, 2005) provides a succinct framework for vocabulary instruction.

1. The teacher explains a new word, going beyond reciting its definition (tap into prior knowledge of students, use imagery).
2. Students restate or explain the new word in their own words (verbally and/or in writing).
3. Students create a nonlinguistic representation of the word (a picture, or symbolic representation).
4. Students engage in activities to deepen their knowledge of the new word (compare words, classify terms, write their own analogies and metaphors).
5. Students discuss the new word (pair-share, elbow partners).
6. Students periodically play games to review new vocabulary (Pyramid, Jeopardy, Telephone).

It is also beneficial to refer to academic vocabulary lists. There are quite a few that can be found on the internet. A list of commonly found academic words that are the result of multiple surveys of textbooks and content area standards is shown in chart 3.1.

What the experts agree on is that students should work with vocabulary in a variety of ways and contexts. Students must manipulate the new words in order to internalize and eventually use new vocabulary in reading and writing.

Strategies for Vocabulary Development through Word Play

DISCUSSION STARTER

When students discuss new words, it facilitates their understanding and considers prior vocabulary terms and concepts. In this strategy, the teacher prompts students to discuss vocabulary words. If a student has a basic knowledge of the word, skip to the next word. There's no need to teach a word if a student has some basic understanding of that word. If the discussion reveals that students do not know the words, create opportunities for them to learn about the new vocabulary *prior* to instruction of a text of new content. You can teach students to learn new vocabulary in some of the following strategies.

abbreviate	cite	cumulative	excerpt
abstract	claim	debate	exclude
according	clarify	deduce	exercise
acronym	class	defend	exhibit
adress	clue	define	explain
affect	code	demand	explore
alter	coherent	demonstrate	expository
alwas	common	depict	extract
analogy	compare	derive	fact
analysis	compile	describe	factor
analyze	complement	detail	feature
annotate	complete	detect	figurative
anticipate	compose	determine	figure
application	composition	develop	focus
apply	conceive	devise	footer
approach	concise	diction	foreshadow
appropriate	conclude	differentiate	form
approximate	conclusion	dimension	format
argue	concrete	diminish	former
argument	conditions	direct	formulate
arrange	conduct	discipline	fragment
articulate	confirm	discover	frame
aspects	consequence	discriminate	frequently
assemble	consider	discuss	general
asert	consist	distinguish	genre
assess	consistent	domain	graph
associate	consistently	draft	graphic
assume	constant	draw	header
assumption	constitutes	edit	heading
audience	consult	effect	highlight
authentic	contend	elements	hypothesize
background	context	emphasize	identify
body	continuum	employ	illustrate
brainstorm	contradict	equal	imitate
brief	control	equivalent	imply
calculate	convert	essay	incline
caption	convey	essential	include
category	copy	establish	incorporate
cause	correlate	estimate	indicate
character	correspond	evaluate	indirect
characteristic	credible	event	infer
characterize	credit	evidence	influence
chart	criteria	exaggerate	inform
chronology	critique	examine	inquire
citation	crucial	example	instructions

Chart 3.1. Academic Vocabulary list

integrate	organize	prose	spatial
intent	origins	prove	pecific
intention	outline	purpose	speculate
interact	pace	quotation	stance
intermittent	paraphrase	quote	standard
inerpret	particpation	rank	state
introduce	passage	rare	statement
introduction	pattern	rarely	strategy
invariably	perform	reaction	structure
investigate	perspective	recall	study
involve	persuade	reduce	style
irony	place	refer	subject
irrelevant	plagerism	reflect	subjective
isolate	plan	regular	subsequent
italics	plausible	relate	substitute
judge	plot	relationship	succinct
key	point	relevant	suggest
label	point of view	rephrase	sum
likely	portray	report	summarize
list	possible	represent	summary
literal	preclude	representative	support
locate	predict	request	survey
logical	prefix	require	symbolize
main	prepare	requisite	synonym
margin	presume	respond	synthesize
mean	preview	responsible	table
measure	previous	restate	technique
metaphor	primary	results	term
method	prior	reveal	test
model	probably	review	theme
modify	precedure	revise	thesis
monitor	process	root	timeline
motivation	produce	rule	tone
narrative	profile	scan	topic
narrator	project	score	trace
never	prompt	sequence	trait
notation	proofread	series	transition
note	property	set	translate
notice	propose	setting	typically
objective	prose	show	unique
observe	prove	signal	utilize
occur	purpose	significance	valid
opinion	prompt	simile	variation
oppose	proofread	skim	vary
optional	property	solve	verify
order	propose	source	viewpoint
			voice

Chart 3.1.   (continued)

FRAYER MODEL

The Frayer model is probably one of the most recognized strategies for vocabulary development. It is a graphic organizer used to develop students' knowledge of a newly introduced word. The students define a vocabulary term and provide examples, non-examples, illustrations, and other activities to prompt students to examine a few words in depth.

There are many adaptations of the Frayer model. A few are illustrated in the following figures.

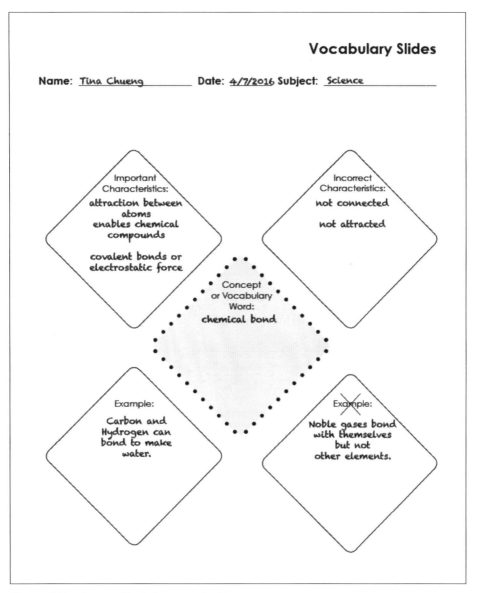

Figure 3.1.   Frayer Model, example 1

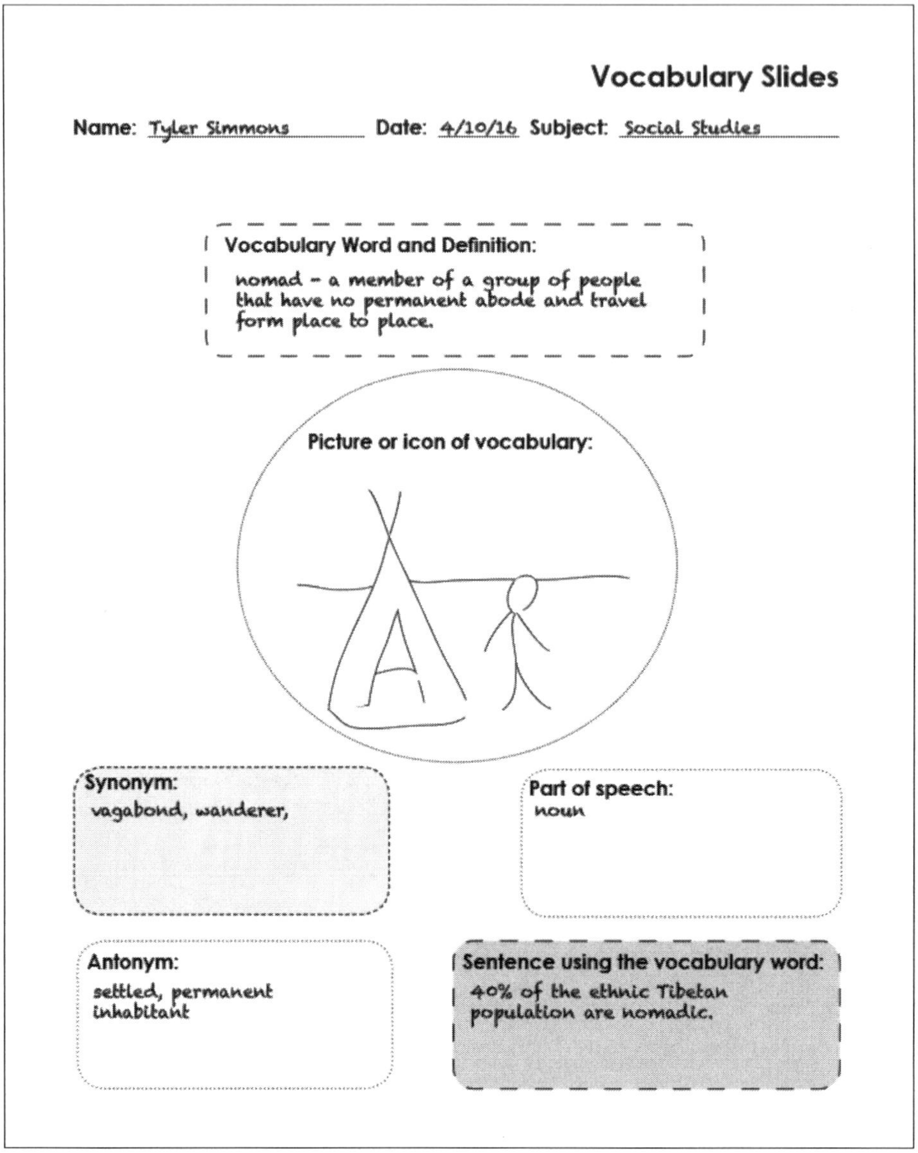

Vocabulary Slides

Name: Tyler Simmons   Date: 4/10/16 Subject: Social Studies

Vocabulary Word and Definition:

nomad - a member of a group of people
that have no permanent abode and travel
form place to place.

Picture or icon of vocabulary:

Synonym:
vagabond, wanderer,

Part of speech:
noun

Antonym:
settled, permanent
inhabitant

Sentence using the vocabulary word:
40% of the ethnic Tibetan
population are nomadic.

Figure 3.2.   Frayer Model, example 2

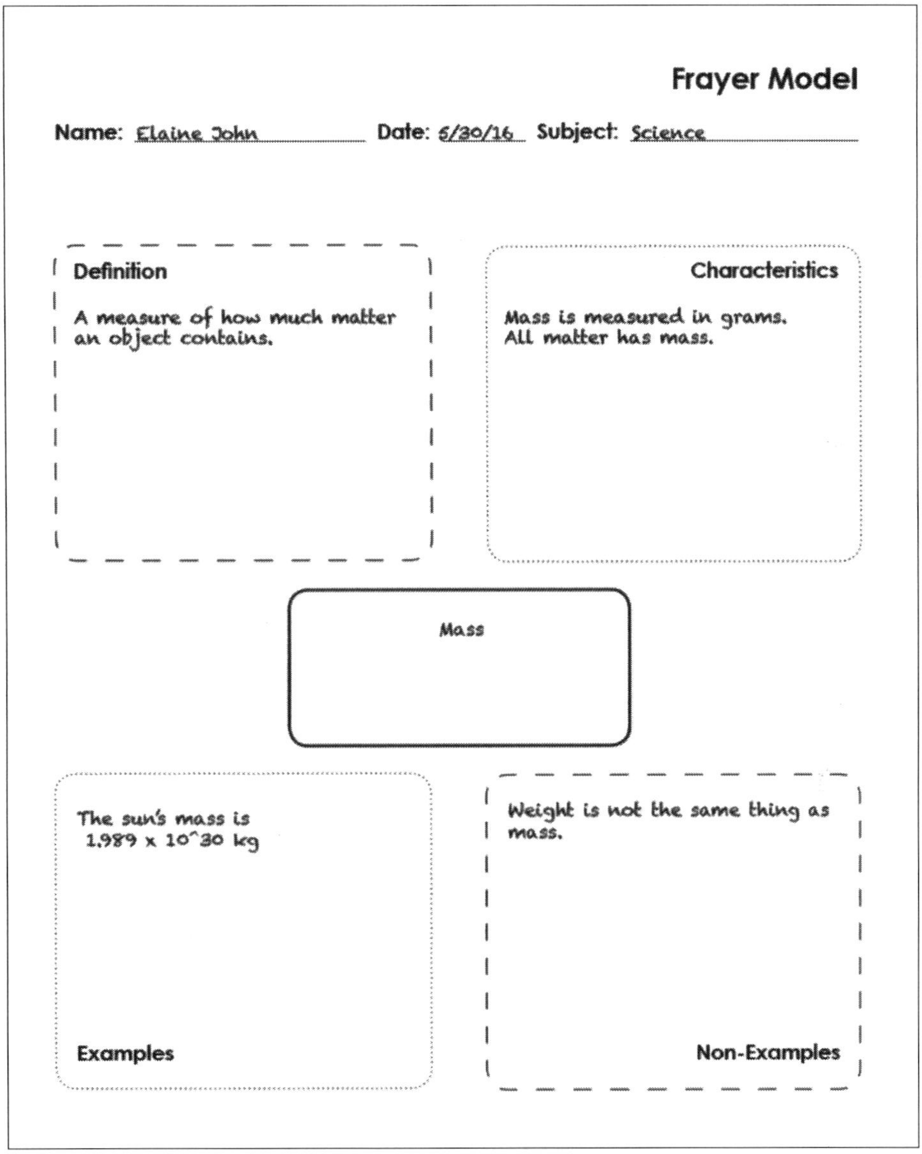

Frayer Model

Name: _Elaine John_   Date: _6/30/16_ Subject: _Science_

Definition

A measure of how much matter an object contains.

Characteristics

Mass is measured in grams.
All matter has mass.

Mass

The sun's mass is
1.989×10^{30} kg

Examples

Weight is not the same thing as mass.

Non-Examples

Figure 3.3.   Frayer Model, example 3

FRONTLOADING VOCABULARY

Introducing key vocabulary prior to the study of new content or reading a new text can facilitate comprehension. A very effective strategy is using the paint chip cards that you might find at a paint store. On the same card, write words that might belong together or different word forms. See the examples that follow.

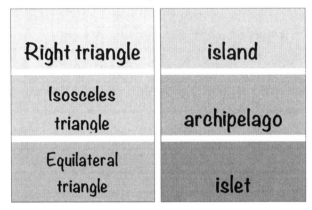

Figure 3.4. Sample of related discipline-specific words for mathematics (right triangle, isosceles triangle, and equilateral triangle) and social studies (island, archipelago, and islet)

Figure 3.5. These vocabulary chips demonstrate shades of meaning with new vocabulary words.

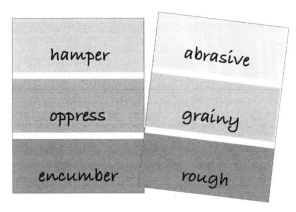

Figure 3.6. Vocabulary chips can also be used for synonyms.

ILLUSTRATION OR PICTIONARY ™

There is much research to support the importance of visualization to foster greater comprehension (Hattie, 2008).

In this vocabulary strategy, students draw pictures to illustrate a vocabulary word from clues that classmates provide. This strategy is conducive to whole group instruction as well as small group. It is best to divide the class into teams of three to four students. One student should be designated as the artist and chooses from a list of words that their classmates cannot see. As the student artist draws the words, the other students guess the vocabulary word.

SEMANTIC FEATURE ANALYSIS

This strategy supports students in understand the meaning of words. When students analyze words and determine the origins and semantic meanings, they are better able to internalize and use the language. The following chart can be used for students to develop their understanding of words through a semantic analysis.

In the far left column, the students or teacher will list the words that are relevant to a specific text or topic. Next, the students should determine if the new word possesses any of the features that are listed across the top of the chart. The students could use symbols like (+) or (−) to indicate corresponding features. Prompt the students to discuss the words and their responses in large group or small group discussion. Remember, it is important for students to discuss words and their meanings. Having students talk about words and language increases their internalization of new vocabulary.

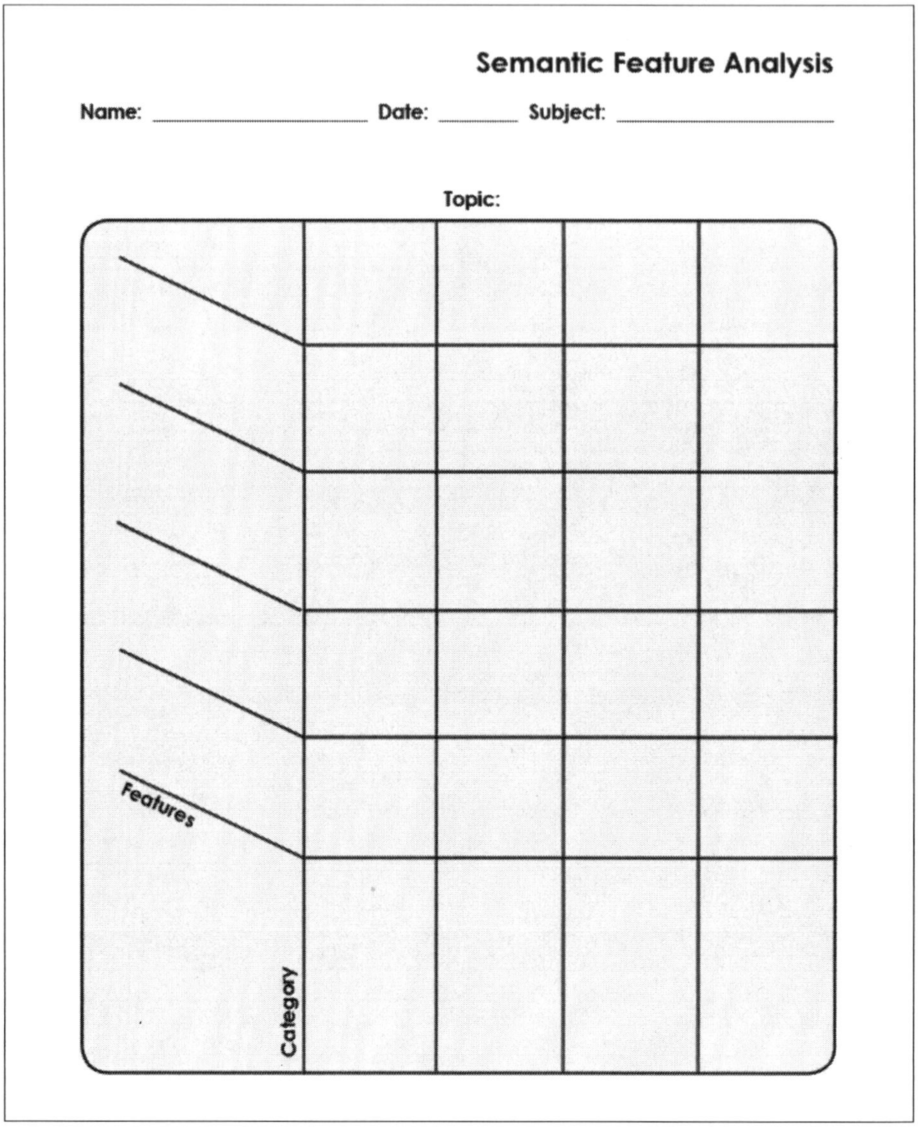

Semantic Feature Analysis

Name: _____ Date: _____ Subject: _____

Topic:

Features

Category

Figure 3.7.   Semantic Feature Analysis template.

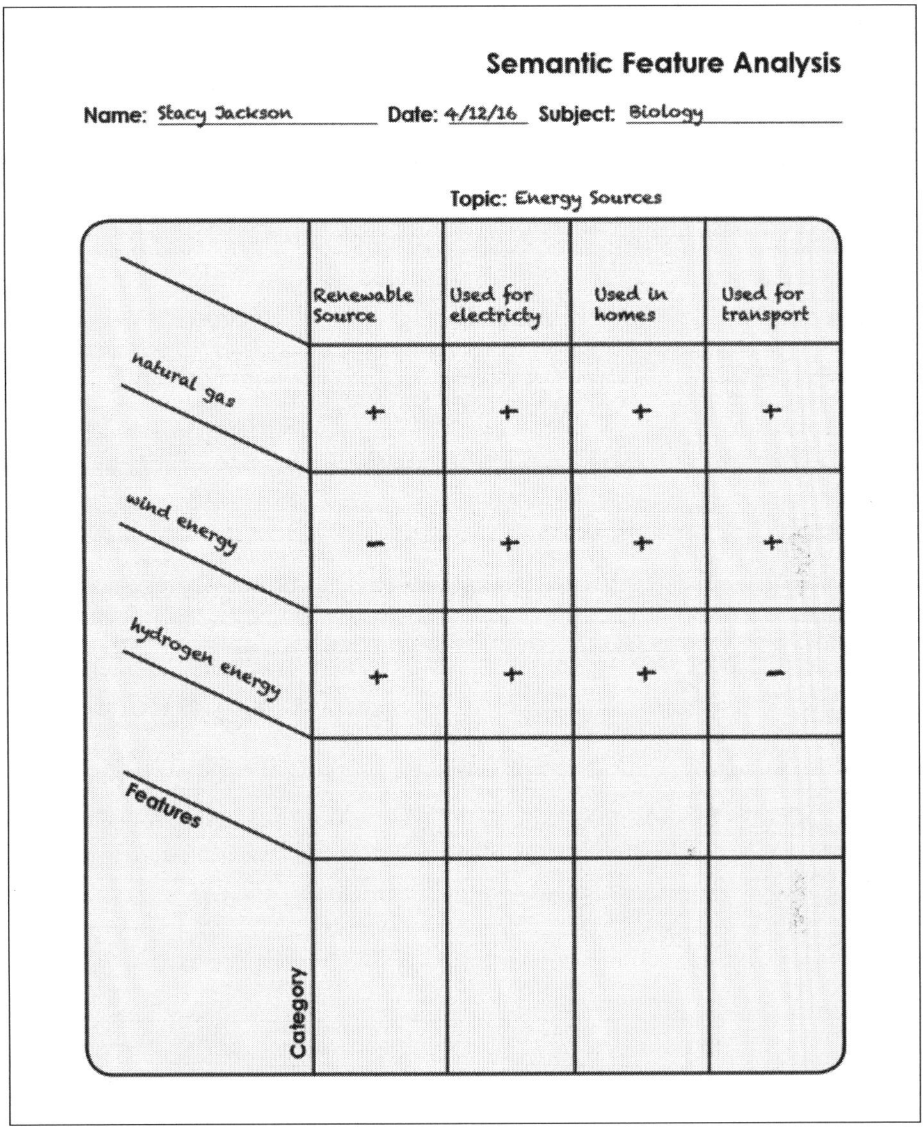

Semantic Feature Analysis

Name: Stacy Jackson _____   Date: 4/12/16 Subject: Biology _____

Topic: Energy Sources

Category	Renewable Source	Used for electricty	Used in homes	Used for transport
natural gas	+	+	+	+
wind energy	−	+	+	+
hydrogen energy	+	+	+	−
Features				

Figure 3.8.   Semantic Feature Analysis student sample

VOCABULARY NOTEBOOKS

Vocabulary notebooks provide students with the opportunity to record words as they strengthen their individual word knowledge and internalize new words. Remember that students need to work and play with new words in order to internalize the new vocabulary. Below are some suggestions for vocabulary notebooks:

• Avoid using dictionary definitions and instead prompt students to create more conversational definitions. Consider giving the students a limit on how many words they can use for their own definitions. When the students have a fixed list of words that they can use for a definition, multiple revisions occur. These revisions reinforce the word and its meaning.

- Instruct students to identify unknown, confusing, or interesting words. The students should write these words in their notebooks.
- Prompt the students to write down the exact sentence in which the identified words occur.
- Next, instruct the students to create a definition for the word. They can reference the dictionary but they must create their own definitions.

Vocabulary Notebooks

Name: _____   Date: _____   Subject: _____

Word and Page Number:

Resource:

Sentence in which the word was used in the text:

Student Friendly Definition:

Antonyms:

Synonyms:

Picture/Drawing/Symbol:

Figure 3.9. Vocabulary Notebooks template

Vocabulary Notebook

Name: Amy Schwart   Date: 9/12/16 Subject: English

Word and Page Number: "expelled" page 219

Resource: Harry Potter and the Order of the Phoenix

Sentence in which the word was used in the text:
"We could all have been killed- or worse, expelled."

Student Friendly Definition:
to kick someone out of something

Antonyms:
absorb, allow, admit, permit, take in

Synonyms:
throw out, eject, bar, ban, remove, dismiss, oust

Picture/Drawing/Symbol:

Figure 3.10. Vocabulary Notebooks student sample

For a few additional ideas try the following:

• Prompt the students to include antonyms and synonyms for each word.
• The students might include a picture or illustration for the word.
• Encourage the students to look for the word in other texts (an internet search is a helpful tool for this activity).

MAGIC SQUARES

Adapted from a Chinese game, this strategy can effectively teach vocabulary:

- Instruct the students to match the lettered column of words with the numbered column of definitions.
- The letters on each square should match the lettered words.
- The students can find the magic number when they successfully match the correct word and definition. They enter the number in the corresponding square on the grid.
- Any number of squares can be used for the puzzle.

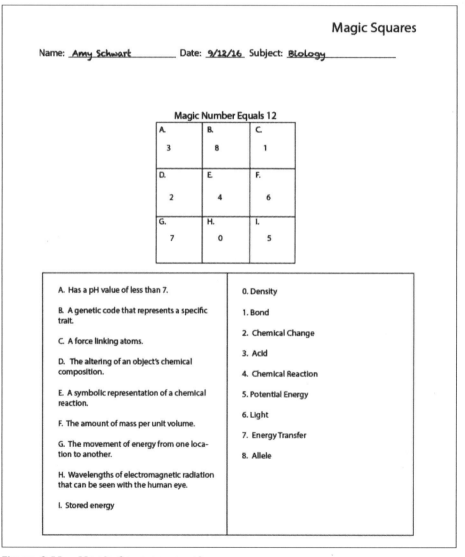

Figure 3.11.   Magic Squares sample

STAR

In this strategy, students learn vocabulary using the STAR (Blachowicz and Fisher, 2014) framework, which is broken down into the following:

S = Select
T = Teach
A = Activate
R = Revisit

To begin, the teacher selects the four to six words that are most essential in understanding a particular text. The teacher draws a story map or text map to illustrate how the words are fundamental to the retelling or understanding of the text. As the teacher teaches these words, be sure to draw on students' prior knowledge about the words and what the words might mean. Next, activate opportunities for the students to use the words in writing and other activities. Finally, it is always necessary to revisit important words. Encourage students to use all of the words that they are learning in writing assignments, in their reading, and through games and other activities.

WORD LISTS AND FAMILIES

Many word lists are available on the internet. These word lists are especially useful for content area teachers. When using a word list, be careful! Make sure that you are being highly selective about the words that you are selecting for your students. A word list should not have more than fifteen words and those selected must be essential for students' understanding of a particular text or topic.

The vocabulary chip activity that was previously described is useful for teaching students about word families. In short, word families contain a root word and the forms of that word. For example:

argue
  argued
    arguing
      argues
        arguable
          arguably

Once students learn the root word, argue, they can also learn about the different forms of that word and how you could use those in various contexts. We are teaching students how to manipulate language in response to different purposes and contexts.

The charts on the next pages list key academic vocabulary words (the lists are not exhaustive).

Word	Noun	Verb	Adjective	Adverb
abstract	abstract abstractionist	abstract abstracts abstracted abstracting	abstractly	
address	address	address addresses addressed addressing	addressable	
affect	affect affection affectivity	affect affects affected affecting	affected	affectively
analogy	analogist analogy analogousness	analogize analogizes analogized analogizing	analogous	analogously
analyze	analysis analyst	analyze analyzes analyzed analyzing	analytic analytical	analytically
annotate	annotator annotation	annotate annotates annotated annotating	annotative	annotatively
apply	applicability	apply applies applied applying	applicable	applicably
approximate	approximation	approximate approximates approximated approximating	approximate	approximately
argue	argument argumentation	argue argues argued arguing	arguable argumentative	arguably argumentatively
articulate	articulate articulation	articulate articulates articulated articulating	articulate	articulately

Chart 3.2.   Key Academic Vocabulary word families

assert	assertion assertiveness	assert asserts asserted asserting	assertive	assertively
associate	associate associates	associate associates associated associating	associative	
calculate	calculator calculation	calculate calculates calculated calculating	calculable calculative	calculatedly
category	category categorization	categorize categorizes categorized categorizing	categorizable categorical	categorically
cause	cause causation	cause causes caused causing	causable causeless causal	causally
chart	chart	chart charts charted charting	charted chartable	
cite	citation citer	cite cites cited citing	citable	
clarify	clarifier clarification	clarify clarifies clarified clarifying	clarifying	
coherent	coherency coherence	cohere coheres cohered cohering	coherent	coherently
compare	comparison comparer comparativeness	compare compares compared comparing	comparative	comparatively

Chart 3.2. (continued)

complete	completeness completion completer	complete completes completed completing	complete completive	completely
compose	composer composition	compose composes composed composing	composed	
concise	concision conciseness		concise	concisely
confirm	confirmation confirmer confirmability	confirm confirms confirmed confirming	confirmed confirmable	confirmingly
consider	considerer consideration	consider considers considered considering	considerate considerable considered	considerably considerately
correlated	correlate correlator correlation	correlate correlates correlated correlating	correlated correlatable correlational	
cumulative	cumulation cumulativeness	cumulate cumulates cumulated cumulating	cumulative	cumulatively
deduce	deductibility	deduce deduces deduced deducing	deductive	deductively
define	definer definability definition	define defines defined defining	definitive	definitively
demonstrate	demonstration demonstrator	demonstrate demonstrates demonstrated demonstrating	demonstrative demonstrable	demonstrably
depict	depiction depictor	depict depicts depicted depicting	depictive	

Chart 3.2. (continued)

		describe		
describe	description describer	describe describes described describing	descriptive	
determine	determination determinism determiner determinist determinedness	determine determines determined determining	determined deterministic	determinedly
develop	development developer	develop develops developed developing	developed developing developmental	developmentally
differentiate	differentiation differentiator	differentiate differentiates differentiated differentiating	differentiated	
discuss	discussion	discuss discusses discussed discussing	discussable	
distinguish	distinguisher	distinguish distinguishes distinguished distinguishing	distinguishing distinguished distinguishable	distinguishably
effect	effect effectiveness		effective	effectively
emphasize	emphasis	emphasize emphasizes emphasized emphasizing	emphatic	emphatically
equivalent	equivalence equivalency		equivalent	equivalently
evaluate	evaluation evaluator	evaluate evaluates evaluated evaluating	evaluative evaluable	
examine	examination examiner examinee	examine examines examined examining	examined examinable examinatorial	examiningly

Chart 3.2. (continued)

explain	explanation explainer	explain explains explained explaining	explanatory explanative	explanatorily
factor	factor factorability	factor factors factored factoring	factorable	
foreshadow	foreshadowing foreshadower	foreshadow foreshadows foreshadowed foreshadowing	foreshadowing	
fragment	fragment fragmentation	fragment fragments fragmented fragmenting fragmentize fragmentizes fragmentized fragmentizing	fragmentary fragmented	
imply	implication	imply implies implied implying	implied	
infer	inference	infer infers inferred inferring	inferable	inferably inferentially
integrate	integration integrator integrationist	integrate integrates integrated integrating	integrated integrating	
interpret	interpretation interpreter	interpret interprets interpreted interpreting	interpretive interpretative interpretational	interpretatively
isolate	isolation isolator isolationist isolationism	isolate isolates isolated isolating	isolated isolating	

Chart 3.2.   (continued)

measure	measure measurement measurability measurer	measure measures measured measuring	measurable	measurably
observe	observation observance observer	observe observes observed observing	observant observable observational	observably observantly
oppose	opposition	oppose opposes opposed opposing	opposing opposable	opposingly
persuade	persuasion persuader persuasiveness	persuade persuades persuaded persuading	persuasive persuadable	persuasively
predict	prediction predictability predictor predictableness	predict predicts predicted predicting	predictable predictive	predictably predictively
prove	provability	prove proves proved proving	proven provable	provably
refer	reference referrer	refer refers referred referring	referable referenced	
represent	representation representative	represent represents represented representing	representational	representationally
respond	response respondent	respond responds responded responding	responsive	responsively
sequence	sequence sequencer	sequence sequences sequenced sequencing	sequensive sequential sequenced	sequentially

Chart 3.2.   (continued)

speculate	speculation speculator	speculate speculates speculated speculating	speculative	speculatively
summarize	summarization summarizer	summarize summarizes summarized summarizing	summarized summarizable	
synthesize	synthesization synthesizer	synthesize synthesizes synthesized synthesizing	synthesized	
translate	translation translatability translator	translate translates translated translating	translated translatable translational	
valid	validity validness	validate validates validated validating	valid	validly

Chart 3.2. (continued)

WORD WALLS

Word walls are an effective tool to develop students' reading and writing vocabularies. In addition, word walls enhance content learning with the introduction of academic language. Word walls also help all levels of readers and English language learners.

The teacher should introduce words to the students as they are encountered in content study. It's best to have a new word written on a large piece of paper and then add it to the word wall. Discuss what the word means and how it is being used in a particular context.

Word walls tend to be most effective when they are interactive. As words are introduced, encourage discussion about the words and perhaps invite the students to create visual representations of the word.

Why Is Vocabulary Instruction So Critical for Reading Success?

There is a substantial body of research that examines the role of vocabulary and language development in learning. As students begin middle school, vocabulary demands substantially increase. When students are exposed to more content-rich texts, they are also required to learn more vocabulary. At the onset of middle school, students delve more into content and the greater depth requires students to learn more vocabulary and terminology. Learning vocabulary matters.

Figure 3.12.   Example of a classroom Word Wall

A student's level of vocabulary directly influences comprehension and learning. Discipline-specific language is also a conduit for conceptual knowledge that occurs more in middle school and high school. When students develop content-specific vocabulary they are more likely to understand the content. In turn, vocabulary knowledge is a strong predictor for reading comprehension. In some studies, it is reported that 70 to 80 percent of reading comprehension is due to vocabulary knowledge (Nagy and Scott, 2000). When our struggling readers still possess challenges with foundational reading skills in middle school and high school as they encounter text that contain increasingly dense, abstract, and technical language with greater frequency, it is no wonder that these students can feel discouraged (Fang, 2008).

THERE IS GOOD NEWS

Vocabulary learning is not about learning definitions. Word knowledge is multifaceted and goes beyond the basic understanding. Learning about synonyms, antonyms, and creating nonlinguistic representations of words develops students' skills in their understanding of how language works and how words can lead to comprehension. There are specific things that we can do in order to improve a student's vocabulary and grow reading comprehension. Specifically,

1. Teach words within the context in which they are found.
2. Use strategies (like the samples featured in this chapter) that require multiple ways to learn and understand new words.
3. Middle school and high school students encounter more challenging texts that demand specific instruction. Students must develop skills in learning new academic vocabulary. Setting aside the instructional time to develop vocabulary skills is critical to student success in their understanding of new concepts and ideas.
4. Encourage students to manipulate and play with new words and vocabulary. When students become more comfortable with words and language, they are more likely to internalize new words and use them in their personal vocabulary.

References

Billmeyer, Rachel. (2003). *Strategies to engage the mind of the learner: Building strategic learners.* Omaha, NE: Dayspring Printing, 42–45.

Blachowicz, Camille L. Z., and Peter Fisher. (2004). Vocabulary lessons. *Educational Leadership* (March), 66–69.

Fang, Z. (2008). Going beyond the fab five: Helping students cope with the unique linguistic challenges of expository reading in the intermediate grades. *Journal of Adolescent and Adult Literacy, 51*(6), 476–487.

Hattie, John. (2008). *Visible learning: A synthesis of over 800 meta-analyses relating to achievement.* New York: Routledge.

Marzano, Robert J. (2004). *Building background knowledge for academic achievement: Research on what works in schools.* Alexandria, VA: ASCD.

Marzano, Robert J., and Debra J. Pickering. (2005). *Building academic vocabulary: A teacher's manual.* Alexandria, VA: ASCD.

McKnight, K. (2014a). *Common core literacy for ELA, history/social studies, and the humanities: Strategies to deepen comprehension.* San Francisco: Jossey-Bass.

McKnight, K. (2014b). *Common core literacy for math, science, and technical subjects: Strategies to deepen comprehension.* San Francisco: Jossey-Bass.

Nagy, N. E., and Scott, J. (2000). Vocabulary processes. In M. L. Kamil, P. B. Mosenthal, P. D. Pearson, and R. Barr (Eds.), *Handbook of reading research* (vol. 3, pp. 269–284). Mahwah, NJ: Lawrence Erlbaum.

Pictionary™. Milton Bradley. East Longmeadow, MA: Milton Bradley Company, 1993.

Richardson, Judy S., and Raymond F. Morgan. (1993). *Reading to learn in the content areas.* Belmont, CA: Wadsworth Publishing Company, 374–375.

Part Two

COMPREHENSION

CHAPTER 4

Fluency Tools
INCREASING COMPREHENSION

When I was first transitioning from an English teacher to a reading specialist, I started hearing about the importance of fluency. Eventually I began working with small groups of struggling secondary students and part of the lesson plan was to have the teacher, me, read a short section, maybe even just a sentence, and have the students read it back just like I did—pause when I paused, make their voices strong when I did, make their voices go up at the end of a question like I just did, and so on. I remember thinking, "This seems babyish and insulting and I doubt it will work, but okay, I'll give it a try." It was like magic. I couldn't believe how powerful it was. Hearing fluent reading and then imitating it gave them a model to emulate when they were reading on their own. I was convinced. Direct fluency instruction is necessary for struggling older readers.

Why We Need to Teach Fluency

Sometimes we assume that our students can already read at a level where they are "reading to learn," but the truth is that many of our students have gaps in their reading skills and there are times when they need us to help them "learn to read." Fluency can be one of those gaps. Along with decoding, fluency affects comprehension and is often thought of as the bridge from decoding to comprehension (Pikulski and Chard, 2005). Disfluent readers have a difficult time constructing that bridge because they are starting and stopping, repeating words or phrases, reading at an incorrect pace, skipping words, and so on. This lack of fluency causes readers to disengage from the meaning. So much of their attention is bogged down on the mechanics of reading that there is little cognitive strength available for comprehension. Sometimes our students can have the decoding knowledge, but they haven't "practiced reading" enough for them to be fluent.

Lisa talks to her students about how reading is a skill, and like any skill, in order to improve you have to practice. She then tells them they are lucky—for she will be their coach and organize their practices. Just like you can't expect to make free throws unless you practice and bend your knees and practice and guide the ball and practice and follow through and practice to get that muscle memory, you must practice to read. You have to practice and notice affixes and practice and read by syllables and practice and automatically recognize sight words and practice to get that metacognitive fluency—to get into the reading flow.

"Ideally, by the time students reach the upper grades, they will have seen hundreds of common words in print many times over, and those words will have become so familiar to them that they can recognize them instantly, in one glance. For instance, instead of decoding 'Mon . . .' and then '. . . day,' they will register the whole word 'Monday' all at once and quickly move ahead with the rest of the sentence" (Heller, *Fluency*). That's ideally. We've all had students who are operating on a less than ideal playing field.

"In a paper on helping students with significant reading comprehension problems, Duke, Pressley, and Hilden (2004) estimate that 75 to 90 percent of students with comprehension difficulties have reading fluency problems that are a significant cause of their comprehension difficulties" (quoted in Rasinski, *Reading Fluency for Adolescents*). As it turns out, direct instruction of fluency isn't babyish or a waste of time—it is essential for students who have difficulties with comprehension.

What Is Fluency?

We can think of fluent reading as having our students read with automaticity (reading words quickly, accurately, and effortlessly), at the proper rate (reading at the proper speed for the task), and with prosody (reading with expression). Fountas and Pinnell (*famous* to elementary teachers) broke this down into six dimensions—pace, pausing, phrasing, stress, intonation, and integration (2006).

PACE

A fast reader does not equal a good reader—we've had that battle with our students many times! Lisa has a student right now who can rattle off all the words very very very quickly, then look up with annoyance because, "Duh, Mrs. Allen—look what a good reader I am!" This same student, however, is unable to tell you much of anything that she just read (which also makes her very mad at Lisa!). She doesn't read with any expression, she blows by all the punctuation, and uses so much cognitive energy on decoding and on speed that she has no space in her brain to pay attention to the meaning.

We've also had students who read at an agonizingly slow pace. All of their brain power is focused on the mechanics of reading—letter-sound, word analysis, and so forth. Often they stop completely to figure out / guess a word or reread a section over a few times until they think they have it right—meanwhile, they're omitting or substituting words and phrases. By the time they get to the end of the paragraph— or sentence!—they have no idea what they just read. Their cognitive energy was so bogged down at the word level, that there isn't space in their brains for the meaning.

PAUSING

It might seem obvious to us, but struggling readers need to be taught to "read the punctuation." They either don't notice it or they don't think it's an important part of reading. Something as simple as prompting them to "make your voice go down at the end of a sentence" can be effective. They know what a question is, they know what a question mark is, but many of them don't know to "make your voice go up at the end of a question." They need reminding to pause slightly at commas and to make their voice sound excited when there is an exclamation mark. Natural speaking has built-in appropriate pauses and high or low tones. Words on a page should be read to make it sound like natural speaking—the punctuation is there for us to follow.

PHRASING

We. Don't. Talk. Word. By. Word. We. Shouldn't. Read. Word. By. Word. Whenwespeak, we speakinphrases. Whenwearereading, weshouldreadinphrases. Punctuation helps with some of the phrasing (pausing at commas, slightly longer pause at the end of a sentence, etc.), but there are other places within a sentence where we can read a phrase. Prepositional phrases are good phrases (we read onthetable, and not, on. the. table), as are compound words (we read lighthouse, not light. house.) and descriptions (we read greenandgold, not green. and. gold.).

STRESS

It's important to teach struggling readers to stress certain words or to make the sentence sound happy or sad depending on the content. If the author has bolded, italicized, or used all caps for a word or phrase, you need to read it like it's important because the author wants it to stand out as different. Even if there aren't any cues, the intended stress can be important to the meaning. Think of the difference between a black′ board (emphasis on black) and a black board′ (emphasis on board).

INTONATION

We don't speak in a monotone. It's easier to understand what we're reading if we vary the tone much like we do when we're speaking. Sometimes we sound loud, sometimes soft. Sometimes we sound excited, sometimes tired. Sometimes we sound friendly, sometimes mean. If we're reading about a sarcastic character, we should make the voice—either out loud or in our heads—sound sarcastic. Lisa had a student once who would test well on a passage he read out loud, but he would do terrible on anything he read on his own. She asked him why he thought this was happening and he said that he can understand it better when he hears it out loud. He would read well and with expression when he was reading something out loud. When he was reading in his head, he said it was just a bunch of words. Lisa then encouraged him to "read out loud inside your head." They would practice that skill every day—it was a little weird because, of course, it was going on silently in his head—he totally would have gotten away with singing "Twinkle, Twinkle Little Star" in his head while Lisa thought he was "reading," but he really did practice and eventually he acquired that skill and began to comprehend much better after silently reading.

INTEGRATION

At first students will need to focus separately on whatever fluency skill or skills they are struggling with—rate, pausing, phrasing, stress, or intonation. Eventually they will be able to integrate all of the fluency components and practice them all at once. The goal is for them to be able to read to make it sound like they're talking, telling a story, or explaining something. As mentioned earlier in this chapter, the "reading words" for this are automaticity, at the proper rate, and with prosody.

Fluency is a skill. If our students haven't developed the skill by the time we get them, they will have a more difficult time reading, learning, and using our content. Isn't that our goal? Like any skill, in order to improve, you need to practice.

How to Practice Fluency

- Read Aloud to Your Secondary Students—Listening to you read fluently gives your students a model of fluent reading to emulate. Read aloud both fiction and nonfiction so they can hear fluent examples of both genres. Find out more about reading aloud in chapter 7.
- Echo Reading—The teacher reads and student(s) copy exactly how the teacher read. Students pause when the teacher paused, make their voices go down when the teacher's voice went down, use an excited voice when the teacher did. Start with a sentence, move to two sentences, and build up to a paragraph.
- Choral Reading—The whole group reads aloud together; the teacher too at first. Eventually, when the teacher feels the students are strong, comfortable, and fluent, he or she will drop out of the reading. If the students falter and can't get it back, the teacher can join in again and then drop out when the students are reading fluently.
- Repeated Reading—Students reread a passage up to four times to improve fluency. These repeated readings can be timed. "Student practice on certain passages generalizes to improved performance across all reading" (Rasinski et al., 2005). That is good news! Just by giving them time to practice repeated reading, the valuable skill of fluency can transfer across all of their reading. "A special kind of practice is called for, however—the kind of repetitive practice that athletes and musicians engage in—rehearsal or repeated reading of a text" (Rasinski, *Reading Fluency for Adolescents*). It's almost like muscle memory; only it's the "reading muscle" we're attempting to strengthen.

- Readers Theater—Students split up or take parts and read sections of text aloud. This can be timed with a stopwatch or recorded on a tablet or other device. Recording them will also time the readings and show students how much their fluency improved from the first attempt (cold read) to the final.

Figure 4.1.   Students watch their Readers Theater performance.

Scripts can be written for content-area learning to motivate and aid in comprehension. Rees and DiPillo (2006) did a study in both urban and suburban settings. They wrote scripts using social studies textbooks. The settings of the scripts included a talk show where rulers of ancient India and Persia were interviewed, a news report with on-the-scene reporters bringing the latest news from ancient India, and a conversation with the townspeople of Mesopotamia about the building of the empire. The students were engaged while they read and reread the scripts—learning along the way. Eventually the responsibility could be shifted to the students to write the scripts themselves—especially older students, adding another layer of authentic learning (*and* you could use the students' scripts with your class next year). There are a number of sources for scripts for teachers who want to get students on their feet right away. Try Aaron Shepard's RT Page (www.aaronshep.com) as a source for either fiction and nonfiction scripts, as well as tips to turn other texts into scripts. Or find scripts by partnering with your school librarian, drama club, or even a local community or professional theater troupe.

- Students Read to Teacher—Have students read a little bit out loud to you each week—even just a paragraph; it's another way to practice. This could be a cold read or a reread.

Figures 4.2a–b.   Two examples of students engaged in classroom Partner Reading. Notice how one student "talks with his hands" while his partner reads aloud.

Figure 4.3.   Five students can simultaneously listen to an audio recording using an inexpensive headphone splitter.

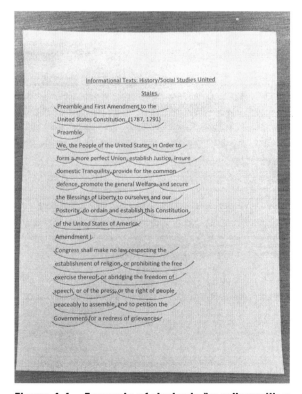

Figure 4.4.   Example of students "reading with a pencil" and scooping the phrases. This example is from appendix B of the CCSS, Text Exemplars, Informational Texts: History/Social Studies.

- Time to Read—A wide range of reading opportunities leads to improved fluency. It's important to arrange time during the day for students to read! You can find time in many different ways:

  Use fifteen minutes of study hall.
  Shift the schedule once a week by three minutes for each class and use the extra time for reading.
  Host a Reader's Workshop in ELA classes once a week.
  Have students read for homework.

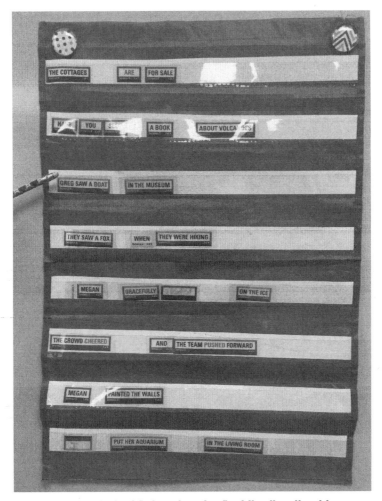

Figure 4.5.   A student "plays teacher" while directing his group to read by phrases. (A confession: those cut-up sentences/ phrases were originally intended for use on an overhead projector. Lisa saved them from samples received while choosing a textbook series years ago. Turns out they work great to practice reading by phrases! Show us someone who saves everything "in case we could use it for something" and we'll show you a teacher!)

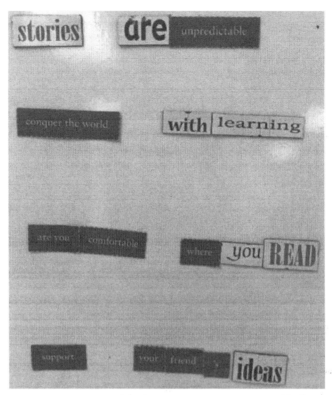

Figure 4.6.   Example of students using magnetic words on a white board to construct phrases.

- Partner Reading—students practice rereading a section of text to each other.
- Audio Assisted Reading—Students read along while listening to a fluent reader.
- Phrased Reading—Students either scoop phrases to read or use cut-up words or transparency sheets to read by phrases. There isn't necessarily an exact "right" way to divide by phrases, but if it sounds awkward, it's probably wrong. Student readers will get a feel for it and as they become more fluent, their phrases will become longer.
- Performance Reading—Students recite or perform poems, song lyrics, chants, monologues, speeches, or excerpts from books. The practice is what builds their fluency.

Assessing Fluency

You may want to assess and keep track of growth for fluency. Fountas and Pinnell (2006) have an excellent rubric to use when assessing fluency. Google "six dimensions fluency rubric" and you'll find a printable, one-page rubric. It breaks all six dimensions of fluency into a 0–3 scale. 0 = almost no evidence of the trait and 3 = almost all of the reading is appropriately fluent for the trait.

You could also score your student holistically (think of Fountas and Pinnell's integration). Some people use a three-point scale: 1 (mostly nonfluent), 2 (mostly fluent), or

End of Grade	Oral Reading Rate (Words Correct per Minute)
1	75-100
2–3	90-120
3	100-140
4	120-160
5	140-180
6	160-200
7–8	180-220

Chart 4.1. Recommended Oral Reading Rates, ©Fountas and Pinnell, Heinemann, 2009. Reprinted with permission.

a 3 (reading fluently). If you score holistically, it is a good idea to decide which dimension caused the breakdown so you know what to practice. Was it rate? Was it stress? This will give you and your student a direction.

Depending on your teaching situation, you may want to track students' oral reading rate over time. Choose a text of at least 200 words, at their independent level, and have them read for a set amount of time—usually between one and five minutes; we suggest starting with one minute. Give a brief introduction to what they'll be reading and have them read it out loud at a comfortable rate. You'll need a copy too, and while they're reading, tally how many words they read correctly in that minute. That is their oral reading rate in words per minute—for that text. See the chart above for targeted reading rate norms recommended by Fountas and Pinnell. You can find other grade level reading rates by other authors, but this is a reference point.

As another reference point—according to an article in *Educational Leadership* by Louisa Moats (2001), adult readers typically read more than three hundred words per minute.

Conclusion

Fluency is a vital component in reading. Most students develop their ability to read fluently while in grade school, but some of our students still need direct instruction and practice. As we stated at the beginning of this chapter, fluency can be thought of as the bridge from decoding to comprehension. If they're too bogged down in the decoding, they won't comprehend, and if they are able to decode but are reading disfluently, they won't comprehend. It is our responsibility to get our content to our students. Helping them become fluent readers will help.

References

Boardman, A. G., Roberts, G., Vaughn, S., Wexler, J., Murray, C. S., and Kosanovich, M. (2008). *Effective instruction for adolescent struggling readers: A practice brief.* Portsmouth, NH: RMC Research Corporation, Center on Instruction.

Deshler, D. D., Hock, M. F., and Catts, H. W. (2006). Enhancing outcomes for struggling adolescent readers. Retrieved from LD Online, http://www.ldonline.org/article/11768.

Duke, N., Pressley, M., and Hilden, K. (2004). Difficulties with reading comprehension. In C. A. Stone, E. R. Silliman, B. J. Ehren, and K. Apel (Eds.), *Handbook of language and literacy: Development and disorders* (pp. 501–520). New York: Guilford

Fountas, I. and Pinnell, G. S. (2006). *Teaching for comprehending and fluency: Thinking, talking, and writing about reading, K–8.* Portsmouth: NH: Heinemann.

Fountas, I. and Pinnell, G. S. (2009) https://www.heinemann.com/fountasandpinnell/supporting materials/oralreadingrates.pdf

Heller, Rafael. *Fluency.* Retrieved from http://www.adlit.org/adlit_101/improving_literacy_instruction_in_your_school/fluency/.

Kamil, M. J. (2003). *Adolescents and literacy: Reading for the 21st century.* Alliance for Excellent Education.

Moats, L .C. (2001). When older students can't read. *Educational Leadership.* 58(6), 36–40.

National Governors Association Center for Best Practices. (2010). Common Core State Standards. Washington DC: National Governors Association Center for Best Practices, Council of Chief State School Officers.

National Institute for Literacy. (2007). *What content-area teachers should know about adolescent literacy.* Washington, DC: The National Institute for Literacy, The National Institute for Child Health and Human Development (NICHD), The U.S. Department of Education's Office for Vocational and Adult Education.

National Institute for Literacy (2007). Adapted from *What Content-Area Teachers Should Know About Adolescent Literacy.* Retrieved from http://www.nifl.gov/nifl/publications/adolescent_literacry07.pdf.

Pikulski, J. J., and Chard, D. (2005). Fluency: The bridge between decoding and reading comprehension. *The Reading Teacher, 58*(6).

Punsalan, M. W. (2006, September). Fluency in the high school classroom: One teacher's method. *Adolescent Literacy in Perspective.*

Rasinski, T. Reading fluency for adolescents: Should we care? Retrieved from http://engagee2ccb.weebly.com/uploads/8/4/6/7/8467476/7.rasinski_reading_fluency_for_adolescents.pdf.

Rasinski, T. V., Padak, N. D., McKeon, C. A., Wilfong, L. G., Friedauer, J. A., Heim, P. (2005). Is reading fluency a key for successful high school reading? *Journal of Adolescent and Adult Literacy, 49*(1), 22–27.

Rees, R., and DiPillo, M. L. (2006, September). Reader's theater: A strategy to make social studies click. Retrieved from Ohio Resource Center: Improving Learning in Ohio website.

Texas Education Agency. (2002). *Fluency: instructional guidelines and student activities.* Retrieved from http://www.adlit.org/article/3416/.

Tyner, B. B., and Green, S. E. (2012). *Small-group reading instruction: Differentiated teaching models for intermediate readers, grades 3–8* (2nd ed.). Newark, DE: International Reading Association.

CHAPTER 5

Active Reading Strategy Tools
EXPANDING COMPREHENSION

Common Core State Standards demand that we raise the level of text complexity for all students. Struggling adolescent readers need to be taught how to comprehend increasingly difficult text. This chapter gives teachers tools for direct instruction of active reading strategies.

David, a seventh grade student, just finished reading an entire passage about photosynthesis from a science textbook. He nails every single word in the passage and "appears" to be reading. However, as soon as he finishes the passage the teacher asks, "Hey David, what's photosynthesis?" David sheepishly tilts his head and shrugs his shoulders. He doesn't know. He can decode anything but he's not engaging in the text and thus is unable to articulate his comprehension of the content.

Does this sound familiar?

Thousands of middle school and high school teachers encounter this scenario every day. What can be done about it? That's a great question. We'll begin to address it in this chapter.

In a nutshell, reading comprehension is about *understanding* a text at both the explicit and inferential level. When we successfully read, we work to understand and learn information as presented in the text. When reading is unsuccessful, our students need to be able to self-monitor and correct their thinking. We talk to them about metacognition, or thinking about their thinking, so they can effectively comprehend text. This chapter contains many strategies and lessons that we have used in middle school and high school classrooms. They are presented here because we have had classroom success with these strategies and instructional approaches. Theory is all well and good but we need ready to use classroom-tested strategies.

Sequence of Events

In this strategy, students are prompted to identify key events in a text, which are indicated by transition words or phrases. The students highlight the transition words and phrases in the texts (see figures 5.1a–c).

HOW DOES THIS STRATEGY DEVELOP COMPREHENSION?

In this strategy students learn to follow the development of ideas and events in a text. It also prompts students to actively seek out key words and phrases that are connectors between ideas, concepts, and events. In essence these transition words and phrases are guides to move the students through the text.

Figure 5.1a.   Sequence of Events activity template

Name:_____

Date:_____

Sequence of Events

Sequence of Events: The order in which events take place. The order can be indicated by transition words or phrases.

For example- before, next, last, after that, on Saturday morning.

Reading the paragraph below, Highlight any transition words or phrases.

History of Relay For Life

In May 1895, Dr. Gordy Klatt walked and ran for 24 hours around a track in Tacoma, Washington to raise money to fight cancer. Throughout the night, friends donated money to run or walk with him. That night, friends donated money to run or walk with him. That single event raised $27,000 for the American Cancer Society. While he circled the track those 24 hours, he thought about how others could take part. He envisioned a 24-hour team relay event that could raise more money to fight cancer. He formed a planning committee and one year later, 340 supporters joined the overnight event. Since those first steps, the Relay For Life movement has grown into a worldwide phenomenon, raising for more than $4 billion to fight cancer. Dr. Klatt's vision for Relay for Life has provided inspiration and hope for millions of cancer survivors and their caregivers. To find a relay event in your area, go to www.relayforlife.org.

Figure 5.1b.   Sequence of Events student sample 1

TIPS FOR INSTRUCTION

Review the transition words and phrases that are listed in figure 5.1a. Explain to the students that authors use transition words as guides for the reader. These words and phrases help readers move along in the text. Then prompt the students to read the passages in figures 5.1b and 5.1c and highlight the transition words and phrases.

Name:_____

Date:_____

Sequence of Events

Sequence of Events: The order in which events take place. The order can be indicated by transition words or phrases.

For example- before, next, last, after that, on Saturday morning.

Reading the paragraph below, Highlight any transition words or phrases.

Vacant Lot Clean Up

It began simply enough: Tim was sick of looking at the mess in the vacant lot he passed on his way home from school. So he started to pick up a piece of trash every afternoon. This didn't seem to make much of a difference, so he began carrying a trash bag and picking up more. Then his friends Mike and Jerry offered to help him. They agreed to clean up the lot on Saturday morning. Next, they put up signs around the neighborhood, announcing the cleanup. Word spread, and on Saturday morning, Tim was amazed to see nearly a dozen people show up to help.

Figure 5.1c.   Sequence of Events student sample 2

Cause and Effect

 Cause and effect is the relationship between why something happened and what happened. Oftentimes, key words or phrases will indicate cause and effect relationships. For example, words and phrases like *because, since, therefore, so, as a result* are signals to the reader that there is a cause and effect relationship.

HOW DOES THIS STRATEGY DEVELOP COMPREHENSION?

Frequently, struggling readers do not use strategies that prompt them to actively engage in the text. Strategies like this develop a student's ability to identify those words that trigger deeper meaning, which are at a more inferential level rather than just at a surface level of comprehension.

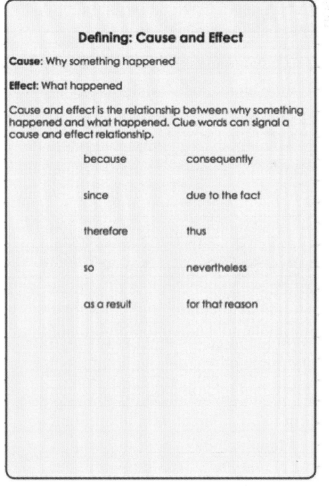

Figure 5.2a.   Defining Cause and Effect

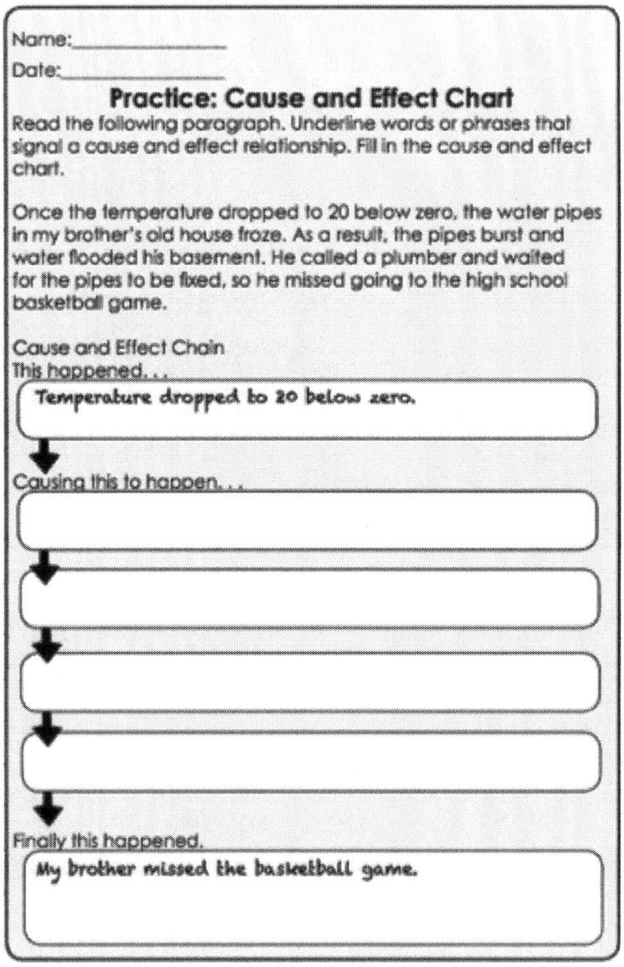

Name:_____

Date:_____

Practice: Cause and Effect Chart

Read the following paragraph. Underline words or phrases that signal a cause and effect relationship. Fill in the cause and effect chart.

Once the temperature dropped to 20 below zero, the water pipes in my brother's old house froze. As a result, the pipes burst and water flooded his basement. He called a plumber and waited for the pipes to be fixed, so he missed going to the high school basketball game.

Cause and Effect Chain

This happened...

> Temperature dropped to 20 below zero.

Causing this to happen...

> [ ]

> [ ]

> [ ]

> [ ]

Finally this happened.

> My brother missed the basketball game.

Figure 5.2b.   Practice: Cause and Effect flow strategy chart

ADDITIONAL PRACTICE FOR CAUSE AND EFFECT

Once students master the event flow strategy you can use the cause and effect chain model. This cause and effect chain model is more complicated since the students do not have prompts and a more structured activity.

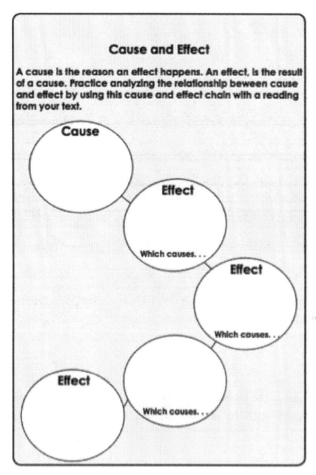

Figure 5.3a. Practice: Cause and Effect chain model

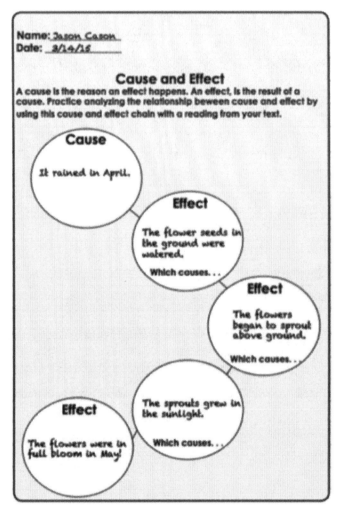

Figure 5.3b.   Practice: Cause and Effect chain model student sample

TIPS FOR INSTRUCTION

Conduct a mini lesson in which the students define the meaning of cause and effect and provide different examples. Explain to the students that there are clue words that can signal a cause and effect relationship and refer them to the list in figure 5.2a.

Symbol

The following activity for identifying the inferential meanings of symbols supports readers to seek more implicit meanings in texts. Students who struggle with comprehension are often stuck on a more literal or concrete level of textual understanding or meaning (see figure 5.4). In this activity, the students are prompted to develop interpretations of concepts or ideas drawn from a concrete object.

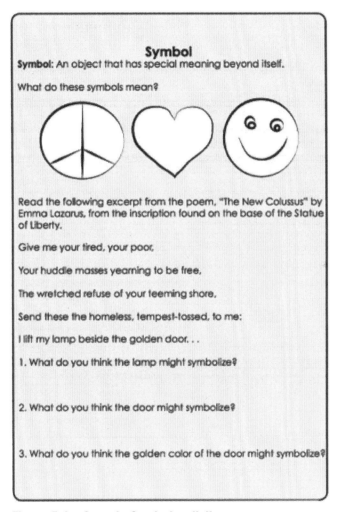

Figure 5.4. Sample Symbol activity

HOW DOES THIS STRATEGY DEVELOP COMPREHENSION?

Frequently, struggling readers do not use strategies that prompt them to actively engage in the text. Strategies like this develop a student's ability to identify words that trigger deeper meaning, at a more inferential level rather than just a surface level of comprehension.

TIPS FOR INSTRUCTION

Share different pictures that portray symbols and ideas. For example, flags from different countries, advertising logos, and emoticons from texting. Discuss how these objects represent meanings and ideas. Next, have the students read the poem "The New Colussus" by Emma Lazarus in figure 5.4 and guide them through the first question, "What do you think the lamp might symbolize?" Once you have completed the first question, instruct the students to complete questions 2 and 3 independently or in student pairs.

Context Clues

 to Context clues are challenging for students, especially when they are assigned increasingly complex discipline-specific text in middle school and high school. In this activity, the students will learn how context clues help readers to guess the meaning of unknown words.

HOW DOES THIS STRATEGY DEVELOP COMPREHENSION?

Proficient readers possess a toolbox of strategies to actively engage with text as a means to increase their understanding and comprehension. One characteristic of struggling readers is that when they encounter a word they don't know, they will either stop reading or skip over the word. One result of this action is that there is a breakdown in student comprehension of the text. Through modeling and practice, students will learn how to identify and use context clues to develop logical guesses for the meaning of newly encountered words.

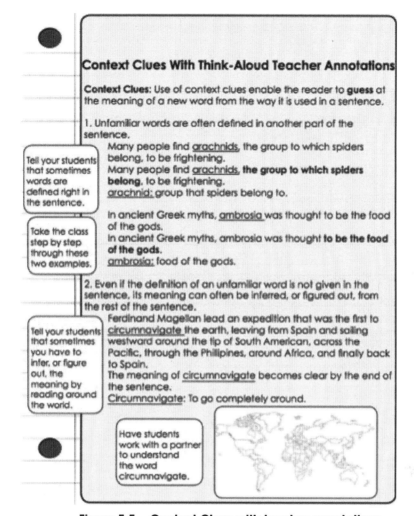

Context Clues With Think-Aloud Teacher Annotations

Context Clues: Use of context clues enable the reader to **guess** at the meaning of a new word from the way it is used in a sentence.

1. Unfamiliar words are often defined in another part of the sentence.

> *Tell your students that sometimes words are defined right in the sentence.*

Many people find arachnids, the group to which spiders belong, to be frightening.
Many people find arachnids, **the group to which spiders belong,** to be frightening.
arachnid: group that spiders belong to.

> *Take the class step by step through these two examples.*

In ancient Greek myths, ambrosia was thought to be the food of the gods.
In ancient Greek myths, ambrosia was thought **to be the food of the gods.**
ambrosia: food of the gods.

2. Even if the definition of an unfamiliar word is not given in the sentence, its meaning can often be inferred, or figured out, from the rest of the sentence.

> *Tell your students that sometimes you have to infer, or figure out, the meaning by reading around the world.*

Ferdinand Magellan lead an expedition that was the first to circumnavigate the earth, leaving from Spain and sailing westward around the tip of South American, across the Pacific, through the Philippines, around Africa, and finally back to Spain.
The meaning of circumnavigate becomes clear by the end of the sentence.
Circumnavigate: To go completely around.

> *Have students work with a partner to understand the word circumnavigate.*

Figure 5.5. Context Clues with teacher annotations

TIPS FOR INSTRUCTION

It is important to model for the students how you use context clues in a text to develop guesses for unknown activities. In a large group think-aloud, demonstrate how you use the information in text as context clues for unknown words. For figure 5.5, annotations are included as a model for this think-aloud.

Figures 5.6a–d contain two additional practice exercises for context clues. Students can practice their context clues skills in pairs or independently.

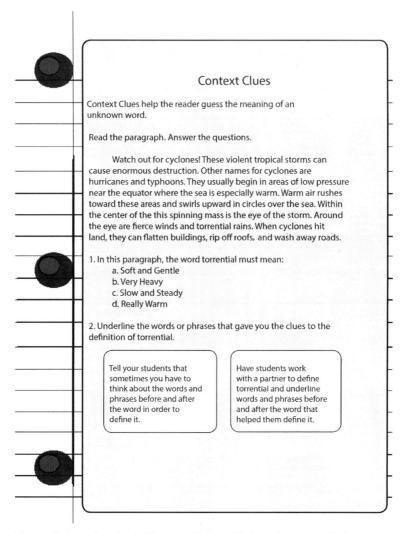

Figure 5.6a.   Context Clues activity with teacher annotations

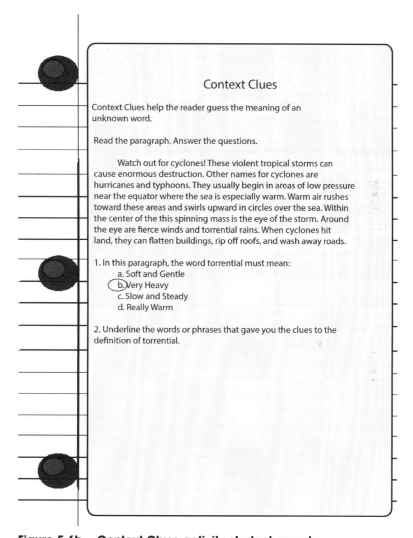

Context Clues

Context Clues help the reader guess the meaning of an unknown word.

Read the paragraph. Answer the questions.

Watch out for cyclones! These violent tropical storms can cause enormous destruction. Other names for cyclones are hurricanes and typhoons. They usually begin in areas of low pressure near the equator where the sea is especially warm. Warm air rushes toward these areas and swirls upward in circles over the sea. Within the center of the this spinning mass is the eye of the storm. Around the eye are fierce winds and torrential rains. When cyclones hit land, they can flatten buildings, rip off roofs, and wash away roads.

1. In this paragraph, the word torrential must mean:
   a. Soft and Gentle
   b. Very Heavy
   c. Slow and Steady
   d. Really Warm

2. Underline the words or phrases that gave you the clues to the definition of torrential.

Figure 5.6b.   Context Clues activity student sample

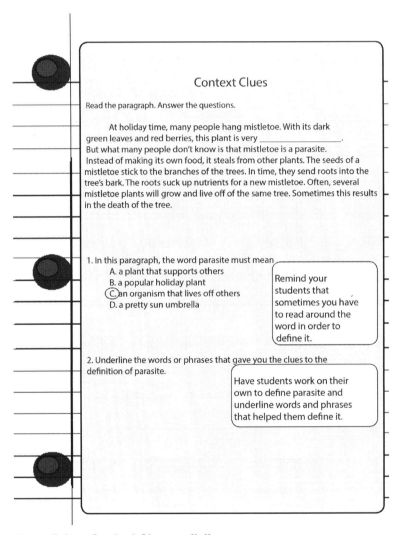

Context Clues

Read the paragraph. Answer the questions.

At holiday time, many people hang mistletoe. With its dark green leaves and red berries, this plant is very _____. But what many people don't know is that mistletoe is a parasite. Instead of making its own food, it steals from other plants. The seeds of a mistletoe stick to the branches of the trees. In time, they send roots into the tree's bark. The roots suck up nutrients for a new mistletoe. Often, several mistletoe plants will grow and live off of the same tree. Sometimes this results in the death of the tree.

1. In this paragraph, the word parasite must mean
   A. a plant that supports others
   B. a popular holiday plant
   C. an organism that lives off others
   D. a pretty sun umbrella

Remind your students that sometimes you have to read around the word in order to define it.

2. Underline the words or phrases that gave you the clues to the definition of parasite.

Have students work on their own to define parasite and underline words and phrases that helped them define it.

Figure 5.6c.   Context Clues activity

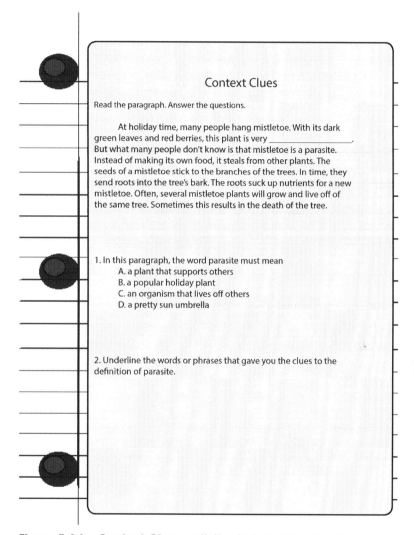

Context Clues

Read the paragraph. Answer the questions.

At holiday time, many people hang mistletoe. With its dark green leaves and red berries, this plant is very _____. But what many people don't know is that mistletoe is a parasite. Instead of making its own food, it steals from other plants. The seeds of a mistletoe stick to the branches of the trees. In time, they send roots into the tree's bark. The roots suck up nutrients for a new mistletoe. Often, several mistletoe plants will grow and live off of the same tree. Sometimes this results in the death of the tree.

1. In this paragraph, the word parasite must mean
   A. a plant that supports others
   B. a popular holiday plant
   C. an organism that lives off others
   D. a pretty sun umbrella

2. Underline the words or phrases that gave you the clues to the definition of parasite.

Figure 5.6d.   Context Clues activity student sample with teacher annotations

Point of View

Point of view is the perspective from which a story is told. A tip for students is to remind them that the point of view is determined by the words in the narration, not the words that are in dialogue. The point of view of a text affects how the reader experiences the events in the story.

Point of View

Point of View (POV): The perspective from which the story is told. Words in narration determine the POV, not the words in dialogue. Point of View affects how the reader experiences the events in the story.

First Person POV
The narrator puts the reader directly in the story.
Not common in literature.

Second Person POV
The narrator puts the reader directly in the story.
Not common in literature.

Third Person POV
The narrator is outside the story.
Pronouns: he, she, they

Read the following selection paying attention to the POV. Who is the narrator?

Figures 5.7a–c.   Point of View activity

Sentry
By Frederic Brown

He was wet and muddy and hungry and cold and he was fifty thousand light-years from home.

A strange blue sun gave light and the gravity, twice what he was used to, made every movement difficult.

But in tens of thousands of years this part of war hadn't changed. The flyboys were fine with their sleek spaceships and their fancy weapons. When the chips are down, though, it was still the foot soldier, the infantry, that had to take the ground and hold it, foot by bloody foot. Like this damned planet of a star he'd never heard of until they'd landed him there. And now it was sacred ground because the aliens were there too. The aliens, the only other intelligent race in the Galaxy. . . cruel, hideous and repulsive monsters.

Contact had been made with them near the center of the Galaxy, after the slow, difficult colonization of a dozen thousand planets; and it had been war at sigh; they'd shot without even trying to negotiate or make peace.

Now, planet by bitter planet, it was being fought out.

He was wet and muddy and hungry and cold, and the day was raw with a high wind that hurt his eyes. But the aliens were trying to infiltrate and every sentry post was vital.

He stayed alert. Gun ready. Fifty thousand light-years from home, fighting on a strange world and wondering if he'd ever live to see home again.

And then he saw one of them crawling toward him. He drew a bead and fired. The alien made that strange horrible sound they all made, then lay still.

He shuddered at the sound and sight of the alien lying there. One ought to be able to get used to them after a while, but he'd never been able to. Such repulsive creatures they were, with only two arms and two legs, ghastly white skins and no scales.

What is the POV of the story?

Who is the narrator?

How did POV effect our experience with the events in the story?

HOW DOES THIS STRATEGY DEVELOP COMPREHENSION?

Understanding point of view and how it works in a text supports students in developing more sophisticated comprehension at an inferential level. Struggling readers tend to understand text on an explicit or surface level. When students develop inferential interpretations of text, they comprehend the text on a deeper level.

The Dinner Party
By Mona Gardner

The country is India. A colonial official and his wife are giving a large dinner party. They are seated with their guests—army officers and government attachés and their wives, and a visiting American naturalist—in their spacious dining room, which has a bare marble floor, open rafters and wide glass doors opening onto a veranda.

A spirited discussion springs up between a young girl who insists that women have outgrown the jumping-on-a-chair-at-the-sight-of-a-mouse era and a colonel who says that they haven't.

"A woman's unfailing reaction in any crisis," the colonel says, "is to scream. And while a man may feel like it, he has that ounce more of nerve control than a woman has. And that last ounce is what counts."

The American does not join in the argument but watches the other guests. As he looks, he sees a strange expression come over the face of the hostess. She is staring straight ahead, her muscles contracting slightly. With a slight gesture she summons the native boy standing behind her chair and whispers to him. The boy's eyes widen: he quickly leaves the room.

Of the guests, none except the American notices this or sees the boy place a bowl of milk on the veranda just outside the open doors.

The American comes to with a start. In India, milk in a bowl means only one thing—bait for a snake. He realizes there must be a cobra in the room. He looks up at the rafters—the likeliest place—but they are bare. Three corners of the room are empty, and in the fourth the servants are waiting to serve the next course. There is only one place left—under the table.

His first impulse is to jump back and warn the others, but he knows the commotion would frighten the cobra into striking. He speaks quickly, the tone of his voice so arresting that it sobers everyone.

"I want to know just what control everyone at this table has. I will count to three hundred—that's five minutes—and not one of you is to move a muscle. Those who move will forfeit fifty rupees. Ready!"

The twenty people sit like stone images while he counts. He is saying ". . . two hundred and eighty. . ." when, out of the corner of his eye, he sees the cobra emerge and make for the bowl of milk. Screams ring out as he jumps to slam the veranda doors safely shut.

"You were right, Colonel!" the host exclaims. "A man has just shown us an example of perfect control."

"Just a minute," the American says, turning to his hostess. "Mrs. Wynnes, how did you know that cobra was in the room?"

A faint smile lights up the woman's face as she replies: "Because it was crawling across my foot."

What is the point of view?

Who is the narrator?

Figures 5.7a–c. Point of View activity

TIPS FOR INSTRUCTION

Begin this strategy with a brief mini lesson that defines point of view and the different types of point of view. This information is included on page 1 of figure 5.7. Next, read aloud the short story, "Sentry" by Frederic Brown with your students. Through a close reading, guide the students to identify and narrator. Next, use the short story, "The Dinner Party" as either a large group activity or as individual practice.

Characterization

HOW DOES THIS STRATEGY DEVELOP COMPREHENSION?

Character traits like physical appearance and attitudes are rarely directly explained or stated in a text. Rather, the character traits are embedded within the text through implicit description, which requires the reader to interpret and draw inferences. This is similar to real life. We have to decipher body language and indirect meanings of written and verbal text. Also the ability for a reader to draw inferences from a text is a

---

Characterization

Characterization: To create a realistic character, writers give details about the character's:

     appearance
     actions
     speech
     thoughts
     what other characters do, say, think about the character

Excerpt from "Thank You, M'am" by Langston Hughes. Fill in the characterization chart for the woman.

     She was a large woman with a large purse that had everything in it but a hammer and nails. It had a long strap and she carried it slung across her shoulder. It was about eleven o'clock at night, and she was walking alone, when a boy ran up behind her and tried to snatch her purse. The strap broke with the single tug the boy gave it from behind. But the boy's weight, and the weight of the purse combined, caused him to lose his balance so, instead of taking off full blast as he had hoped, the boy fell on his back on the sidewalk, and his legs flew up. The large woman simply turned around and kicked him right square in his blue-jeaned sitter. Then she reached down, picked the boy up by his shirt front, and shook him until his teeth rattled.
    After that, the woman said, "Pick up my pocketbook, boy, and give it here."
    She still held him. But she bent down enough to permit him to stoop and pick up her purse. Then she said, "Now ain't you ashamed of yourself?"
    Firmly gripped by his shirt front, the boy said, "Yes'm."
    The woman said, "What did you want to do it for?"
    The boy said, "I didn't aim to."
    She said, "You a lie!"
    By that time two or three people passed. Stopped, turned to look, and some stood watching.
    "If I turn you loose, will you run?" asked the woman.
    "Yes'm," said the boy.
    "Then I won't turn you loose," said the woman. She did not release him.
    "I'm very sorry lady, I'm sorry," whispered the boy.
    "Um-hum! And your face is dirty. I got a great mind to wash your face for you. Ain't you got nobody home to tell you to wash your face?"
    "No'm," said the boy.
    "Then it will get washed this evening," said the large woman starting up the street, dragging the frightened boy behind her.

Figures 5.8a–b. Characterization activity

high-level comprehension skill that is characteristic of higher-level readers. Struggling readers benefit when we directly point this out to them.

TIPS FOR INSTRUCTION

Begin this lesson by explaining that authors aren't going to give us a list of character traits for each character in the story. Writers let us know about a character by how they look, what they do, what they say, what they're thinking, and by telling us what other characters do, say, or think about the character.

Characterization

Name: _____ Date:_____

Learn about a character in a story by finding details about the character's appearance, actions, speech, thoughts and what other characters do, say, or think about the character.

Title:_____ Character:_____

Characteristics	Details from the text	What does this tell us?
What does the character look like?		
What does the character say and do?		
What thoughts and feelings does the character have?		
How do other characters react to the character?		
How would you describe the character?		

Figures 5.8a–b. Characterization activity

Hyperbole

HOW DOES THIS STRATEGY DEVELOP COMPREHENSION?

Struggling readers tend to focus on explicit and literal meanings. Like characterization, a reader must draw inferences from hyperbolic language to determine the author's meaning. In this strategy, the teacher would model for the students how to think about the hyperbolic language. Through a think-aloud the teacher would model how he interprets the author's deeper meaning of the text.

Hyperbole

Hyperbole: Extreme exaggeration. Not meant to be taken literally. Used to emphasize an idea or to be funny.

Read the following excerpt from "Painful Memories of Dating" by Dave Barry. Look for hyperbole and underline it.

> Starting in about 8th grade, my time was divided as follows:
> Academic Pursuits: 2%
> Zits: 16%
> Trying to Figure Out How to Ask Girls Out: 82%
>
> The most sensible way to ask a girl out is to walk directly up to her on foot and say, "So you want to go out or what?" I never did this. I knew that there was always the possibility that the girl would say no, thereby leaving me with no viable option but to leave Crittendon Junior High School forever and go into the woods and become a bark-eating hermit whose only companions would be the gentle and understanding woodland creatures.
> "Hey, Zitface!" The woodland creatures would shriek in cute little Chip 'n Dale voices while raining acorns upon my head. "You wanna date? Hahahohahah!"

Explain why this is hyperbolic.

Figure 5.9.   Hyperbole activity (David Barry, "Oh, He's a Crude Oper-a-Ter: Painful Memories of Dating." *Chicago Tribune*, 22 Mar. 1992)

TIPS FOR INSTRUCTION

In this think-aloud activity, the teacher would read the first passage out loud in class and underline the hyperbole. Through large group discussion, the students and teacher would determine the deeper meaning of the author's language. Next, the students practice with another passage. This practice can be done in pairs or independently.

Making Predictions

HOW DOES THIS STRATEGY DEVELOP COMPREHENSION?

What we already know about struggling readers is that they usually don't question or make predictions while they're reading. They are stuck in the immediate moment of the text and rarely "think ahead." Predicting and confirming or changing predictions leads to active reading. When students are actively reading, their comprehension dramatically improves.

TIPS FOR INSTRUCTION

In this activity, there are three passages. Through an "I do, we do, you do" instructional approach, the teacher should read aloud and model how she makes a prediction based on the evidence in the text. For the next passage, put the students in pairs. The students will read this aloud together and make a prediction about the text. Finally, prompt the students to create an independent prediction with the third passage.

Making Predictions

Making Predictions: Using details from the text and your experience to make a prediction about what will happen.

Read the following short scenarios. Consider the details from the text and add them to what you already know about the world and make a prediction. It's okay if it is wrong, just as long as you can support your prediction with details/experience.

1. Tim, Pat and Sharon put on their snowsuits. They got their hats, boots and scarves. They went outside and began to roll the snow into three large snowballs. They put the largest one on the bottom, then came the next largest and finally, the smallest was on the top of the stack. They went to look for sticks.

Make a prediction:

> After you do this as a mini lesson, find suitable passages from text the students are reading.

2. Linda and her mom drove to the computer store. Linda had the money she received for Christmas and the money she had saved. She waited a long time for this day. Finally, it was going to be convenient to look up all the things she needed for school and to go on Facebook and Twitter.

Make a prediction:

3. The storm began suddenly. The lightning lit up the sky and the thunder roared loudly. The electricity was blinking on and off.

Make a prediction:

Figure 5.10.   Making Predictions activity with teacher annotations.

Allusion

HOW DOES THIS STRATEGY DEVELOP COMPREHENSION?

Similar to predictions, struggling readers tend to be literal and passive when they are reading. Since allusions are unexplained references, struggling readers will often give up if they don't understand what the author is referring to. When an author uses allusions, they assume that the reader has prior knowledge (or schema) for that reference.

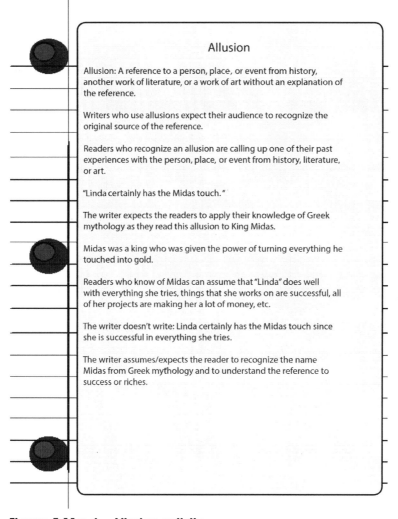

Figures 5.11a–d.   Allusion activity

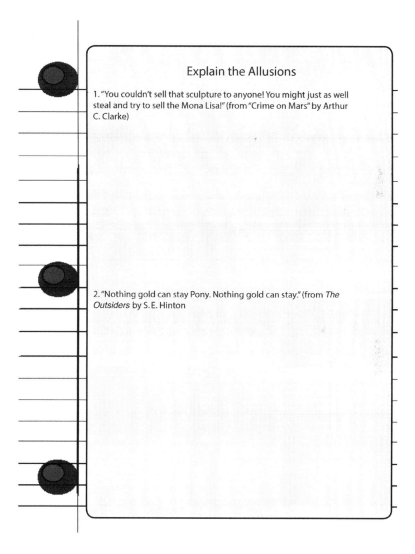

Explain the Allusions

1. "You couldn't sell that sculpture to anyone! You might just as well steal and try to sell the Mona Lisa!" (from "Crime on Mars" by Arthur C. Clarke)

2. "Nothing gold can stay Pony. Nothing gold can stay." (from *The Outsiders* by S. E. Hinton

Figures 5.11a–d.   Allusion activity

TIPS FOR INSTRUCTION

For this activity, the Midas and Mona Lisa allusions are ones that the students should be able to identify with relative ease. The third allusion is embedded within a poem and is more challenging. Depending on your students' proficiency, you may want to model how you identify allusions and then allow the students to practice with allusions in examples two and three.

> **May 3, 2012**
>
> **New York (CNN)** -- As construction workers cheered, the final two pieces of a 408-foot spire were hoisted high about their heads Thursday to the top of One World Trade Center.
>
> Draper with the American flag, the silver spire settled on a temporary platform. Final installation of the pieces will happen later.
>
> "(It's a) beacon that'll be seen for miles around and give a tremendous indication to people around the entire region, and the world, that we're back and we're better than ever," said Steven Plate, director of construction, CNN affiliate WABC reported.
>
> Once the building is complete, it will stand at a height of 1,776 feet. An **allusion** to the birth of the nation.

Explain how 1776 is an allusion.

Author's Purpose in Poetry

HOW DOES THIS STRATEGY DEVELOP COMPREHENSION?

Like the other activities in this chapter, understanding the author's message in poetry is challenging for struggling readers because it is not explicit. The nature of poetry as a genre comprises deep inferential meanings that the reader must be willing to interact and engage with in the text.

Author's Purpose in Poetry

Author's purpose: What the author wants to accomplish by writing
   To entertain by telling a story
   To inform/explain about something
   To Persuade you to think a certain way
   To describe an experience

The thoughts poets express and the language they use are designed to appeal not only to the readers' reasoning, but also to their emotions.

Read the following poem and try to determine Emily Dickinson's purpose for writing.

If I Can Stop
by, Emily Dickinson

If I can stop <u>one heart from breaking</u>
<u>I shall not live in vain;</u>
If I can ease <u>one life</u> the aching,
Or cool <u>one pain,</u>
Or help <u>one fainting robin</u>
Unto his nest again.
<u>I shall not live in vain.</u>

1. What do you think Dickenson's purpose for writing this poem was?
Every small kindness counts/is important.

2. What details from the poem support this purpose?
The repetition of the word "one".

3. What emotions do you think Dickenson is trying to appeal to?
Love, kindness, generosity etc.

Figures 5.12a–b. Author's Purpose in Poetry

Author's Purpose in Poetry

Author's purpose: What the author wants to accomplish by writing
   To entertain by telling a story
   To inform/explain about something
   To Persuade you to think a certain way
   To describe an experience

The thoughts poets express and the language they use are designed to appeal not only to the readers' reasoning, but also to their emotions.

Read the following poem and try to determine Emily Dickinson's purpose for writing.

If I Can Stop
by, Emily Dickinson

If I can stop one heart from breaking
I shall not live in vain;
If I can ease one life the aching,
Or cool one pain,
Or help one fainting robin
Unto his nest again.
I shall not live in vain.

1. What do you think Dickenson's purpose for writing this poem was?

2. What details from the poem support this purpose?

3. What emotions do you think Dickenson is trying to appeal to?

TIPS FOR INSTRUCTION

For this activity, prompt the students, with your guidance, to identify the author's purpose. Ask your students, "Why did the author write this poem?" Or "What does the author want us to learn or think about?" Depending on your students' proficiency, you may want to model how you identify author's purpose and then allow the students to practice with the example in figure 5.12b.

Figurative Language

HOW DOES THIS STRATEGY DEVELOP COMPREHENSION?

When students understand figurative language with ease, they comprehend text at a more sophisticated level. Therefore, with struggling readers, we must provide substantial practice with interpreting the meaning of implicit language. Consider boosting your students' confidence by saying to struggling readers, "Hey, you know that if you said this to a first grader they wouldn't understand it. The first graders don't have the reading experiences and brain power that you do."

Figurative Language

Figurative Language: Sometimes writers use words beyond their ordinary meaning. It is called figurative language. It requires that you use your imagination to figure out what it means.

Read the sentences below. The author does not intend for you to take them literally (actually, exactly what it says). Figure out what the author means and write it in the Literal Meaning column.

Figurative Language	Literal Meaning
It's raining cats and dogs!	
She is a walking calculator!	
Let's cross that bridge when we come to it.	
He was on cloud nine when he won.	
Time to hit the hay!	

Figures 5.13a–b.   Figuration Language activity

TIPS FOR INSTRUCTION

Consider beginning this lesson with the question, "What does the term *literally* mean?" The students are likely to chuckle, of course, as they provide some responses. Then prompt them by asking, "What do you think the author *meant* by that statement?" As the students discuss ideas they'll begin to recognize that authors and text are not always literal. Especially in literary texts, the author uses implicit language to create sensory responses from their readers.

Some Additional Thoughts about this Chapter

Do you remember when we discussed the four components (alphabetics, fluency, vocabulary, and comprehension) of reading? Once the students have mastered automatic decoding, one of the greatest challenges for our readers is that they have great difficulty in determining the meaning of text that does not contain literal meanings. The lessons and strategies in this chapter are designed to support students to develop their ability to look beyond the literal meaning of a text and delve into the more interpretive and deeper meanings of text.

References

Blachowicz, C. L. Z., and Fisher, P. (2004). "Vocabulary Lessons." *Educational Leadership*, *61*(6), 66–69.

Clarke, A. C. (2000). *The collected stories of Arthur C. Clarke*. New York: Tom Doherty Associates, LLC.

Dickinson, E. (1924). "Part One: Life. VI." *Complete Poems*. Retrieved from http://www. bartleby.com/113/1006.html.

Fang, Z. (2008). Going beyond the Fab Five: Helping students cope with the unique linguistic challenges of expository reading in the intermediate grades. *Journal of Adolescent and Adult Literacy, 51*(6), 476–487.

Hattie, J. (2008). *Visible learning: A synthesis of over 800 meta-analyses relating to achievement*. London: Routledge.

Marzano, R. J. (2004). *Building background knowledge for academic achievement: Research on what works in schools*. Alexandria, VA: ASCD.

Marzano, R. J., and Pickering, D. J. (2005). *Building academic vocabulary: A teacher's manual*. Alexandria, VA: ASCD.

Nagy, N. E., and Scott, J. (2000). Vocabulary processes. In M. L. Kamil, P. B. Mosenthal, P. D. Pearson, and R. Barr (Eds.), *Handbook of reading research*, 3, 269–284.

Richardson, J. S., and Morgan, R. F. (1999). *Reading to learn in the content areas*. Belmont, CA: Wadsworth Publishing Company.

CHAPTER 6

Read-Alouds

MODELING FLUENT READING

I have read Where the Red Fern Grows *by Wilson Rawls out loud many, many times. In case you didn't know, there are some very, very sad parts. It's such a great read-aloud though, so I have figured out a way to read through the sad parts without crying or getting choked up. While reading the words, with all the emotion and expression that is called for, I think of something else. Once while I was reading one of the sad parts I was distracting myself by thinking about my plans for after school that day. I won't give away anything in the plot in case you haven't read it, but that day I looked up and I saw two eighth grade boys crying in the front row. Two! One was trying to tip his head back ever so slightly so nobody behind him noticed while he blinked the tears way, but the tears came out anyway. The other one already had his head cradled in the crook of his elbow on the table and he'd ever so slightly wipe his tears on his sleeve with his other hand. Both boys were barely moving and listening intently. Well, I completely lost it. I got choked up and the tears came out of my eyes. They made me cry! I was saying the words I'd said many times while thinking, "OK, I'll stop for gas and then go to the store to pick up milk." I saw these two "tough" eighth grade boys cry in school and it hit me. Wiping my tears I said, "Wow! I've read this book a million times! I knew this was coming! I don't know why I'm crying this time!" While the class was focused on me, the boys gathered themselves and then joined in on the good-natured teasing from the class. Each boy knows I saw him—I'm not sure if they know about each other or not, and they know I didn't say anything. Taking the time to read aloud is worth it.*

"Reading aloud is the best advertisement because it works. It allows a child to sample the delights of reading and conditions him to believe that reading is a pleasurable experience, not a painful or boring one" (Trelease, 2013).

Jim Trelease is the king of reading aloud. He published his first *Read-Aloud Handbook* in 1982 and published the seventh and final edition in 2013. We highly recommend it. The information and advice about reading aloud starts from birth, but he does address reading aloud to older students. He includes a "Treasury of Read-Alouds" at the end of his book that includes picture books, fairy tales, short novels, novels, poetry, and anthologies. Trelease's website has an abbreviated version of the

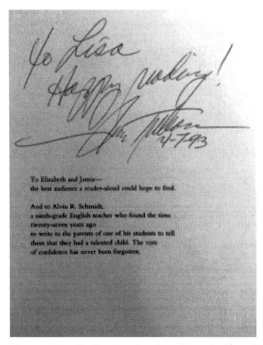

Figure 6.1.   As the inspired and inspirational Jim Trelease reveals in the dedication of his *Read-Aloud Handbook*, teachers and read-alouds can have a profound impact.

treasury to get you started. His work helped to begin a conversation about the efficacy of reading aloud (Trelease, 2017).

The 1985 landmark report *Becoming a Nation of Readers* states that "the single most important activity for building the knowledge required for eventual success in reading is reading aloud to children" (Anderson et al., 1985). Although some of the terms have changed over time, for example, "readability formulas" are now "text complexity," the report "continues to be a summary of a vital era of research on reading processes and texts . . . worthy of attention" (Hiebert, 2013). There have been subsequent national reports including *Teaching Children to Read*, a report of the National Reading Panel (2000), that established the power and importance of reading aloud.

Reading Aloud to Older Students

READING ALOUD GIVES THEM A POSITIVE
EXPERIENCE WITH A BOOK

Let's face it. Many of our adolescent students have never read an entire book. For whatever reason—lack of skill, time, interest, availability, whatever—they've never read a book cover to cover, and some are pretty open and proud about it and declare,

"Reading is supid!" In our experience, there has never been a student who has not enjoyed at least one book read aloud. Whatever the obstacle or is for our students, reading aloud provides positive experiences for these struggling readers. They begin to develop the mind-set that reading is good. Sharing a compelling, enjoyable, important, interesting, or funny book with their classmates is powerful. They start to trust that it can happen—that reading *can* be a good thing. They begin to trust their teacher and that maybe this class and reading is not stupid. One year, the teacher across the hall from Lisa happened to be in her room in-between classes and noticed a student who didn't have the greatest reputation for academics or behavior rush to reach into the podium to quickly go to the bookmark for his class and try to catch himself up on Louis Sachar's *Holes* because he missed the read-aloud the day before while he was at in-school suspension. That teacher was convinced. It's worth the class time and she's been reading aloud to her classes ever since.

READING ALOUD EXPOSES THEM TO BOOKS, GENRES, AUTHORS, AND TOPICS

"Reading aloud can advance teens' listening and literacy skills by piquing their interest in new and/or rigorous material" (Hinds, 2015). Typically a person's listening comprehension is higher than their reading comprehension; therefore, reading aloud is an effective way to encourage students to think outside the box and take on a challenge.

Secondary teachers can read poetry in their classes. It can be a fun way to introduce a topic. The following excerpt from a book of poems called *Science Verse* by Jon Scieszka and Lane Smith (2004) could be used to introduce the states of matter.

> "What's the Matter?"
> Miss Lucy had some matter.
> She didn't know its state.
> She only had three choices,
> So tried to get it straight.
>
> She thought it could be liquid,
> Quite possibly a gas,
> And if it wasn't solid,
> Well call me sassafras.

(From *Science Verse* by Jon Scieszka and Lane Smith,
Viking Books for Young Readers. Reprinted with permission.)

Silly? Sure, the whole book is silly, but it could hook your students.

Secondary teachers can read children's books in their classes. Reading aloud could also be used for an introduction, but there are many sophisticated "children's books" that can be the catalyst for deep discussions about the topics we teach. The following is an excerpt from *Pink and Say*, by Patricia Polacco, that could be read during a Civil War unit. It is based on a true story about two young soldiers—one white and one "mahogany"—and we challenge you to read it out loud to your classes without getting a little teary (we can't do it).

> Then fever must have took me good, 'cause I could feel a cool, sweet-smelling quilt next to my face. Soft, gentle warm hands were strokin' my head with a cool wet rag cloth.
>
> "Look at that mornin' that's comin'," a woman's voice said as she spooned oat porridge into me. "Do your mama know what a beautiful baby boy she has?"
>
> "Where am I? Is this heaven?" I asked.
>
> She tossed her head and laughed. "No child, Pinkus brung you home to me—don't you remember?"
>
> The mahogany child, I thought.
>
> "Both you children been on the run for days, and a miracle of God Almighty brung you both here, yes indeed, child, a miracle."
>
> I remember thinkin', Could this war have been so close to this lad's home? I couldn't imagine havin' a war right in his back yard. I looked over and saw him lookin' out the winderlight.
>
> "Guess you don't remember much," he said. "I'm Pinkus Aylee, fought with the Forty-eighth Colored. Found you after I got lost from my company."
>
> "My name is Sheldon. Sheldon Curtis," I said weakly.
>
> "This is my mother, sweet Moe Moe Bay," he said as she smiled at me.

(From *Pink and Say* by Patricia Polacco, Philomel Books. Reprinted with permission.

Secondary teachers can read short newspaper, magazine, or online articles aloud to spark real-world conversations and thinking about our content. Many of our students don't have the time and many don't have the inclination or even the skills to read something that wasn't assigned. If we model how to read outside of school—in our topics or just in general, we are doing a great service to our students by teaching them how to become informed citizens.

READING ALOUD FROM A SERIES WILL ENCOURAGE STUDENTS TO READ THE REMAINING BOOKS ON THEIR OWN

When the dystopian book craze started, Lisa read the *Hunger Games* by Suzanne Collins (2010) out loud to her high school students (freshman and sophomore). They loved it. In fact, one of her students shocked her parents by asking for a copy of *Catching Fire* (second in a series of three titles) as a gift so she could read along. Eventually she read ahead; it raised her excitement and mind-set for reading.

The students were wild for the genre, so when her class finished that series, Lisa read the first book in the *Uglies* series by Scott Westerfeld. She got smart though and only read the first one and then made the second one available for them to read on their own. They did.

The magic doesn't just happen with dystopian series. Lisa has had success having students read on in the Maximum Ride series by James Patterson (fantasy, book one *The Angel Experiment*), the Alex Rider series by Anthony Horowitz (spy novels, first book *Stormbreaker*), the Ascendance Trilogy by Jennifer A Nielsen (historical fantasy, first book *The False Prince*), and the Percy Jackson and the Olympians series by Rick Riordan (fantasy based on Greek mythology, first book *The Lightning Thief*).

READING ALOUD PROVIDES THE OPPORTUNITY TO DISCUSS LIFE CONCERNS AND BUILDS A SENSE OF COMMUNITY

Our older students face a lot of confusing issues and messages about life and the world every day. Discussing it around a character or a situation in a book can be a safe, comfortable place to talk about dangerous, uncomfortable topics. Laurie Halse Anserson's 2009 book *Wintergirls* brings out into the open the life and death realities of eating disorders. It is painful to read, but the pain is real and the students know it.

Lisa reads *On My Honor* by Marion Dane Bauer to her students just about every year. The boys in the story are eleven, but Lisa has them become the age (or very close to the age) of the group Lisa is reading to by changing their age when she reads that part out loud. This book lends itself to amazing discussions about (not giving anything away) personal responsibility and blame. What should *you* do about peer pressure—giving and/or receiving, intended and/or unintended?

Reading aloud R. J. Palacio's novel *Wonder* provides an occasion to "get to know" a kid with a rare medical facial deformity who is forced to deal with bullies in middle school. Your students will not only get to know Auggie, but they will love him and want to be his best friend. The life lessons and discussions about the power of bullying *and* the power of being brave and kind are incredible. One of Lisa's favorite memories of reading this book aloud is after a particularly kind gesture in the story, one of her students instantaneously pushed his chair back, threw his arms in the air, and yelled "OK—this is now officially my favorite book!" Then he looked around at everyone, pushed his chair in saying, "Sorry, sorry, sorry." The whole class was smiling and saying things like "me too" and "no, I get it," and "it's my favorite book too." Powerful stuff.

READING ALOUD TO OLDER STUDENTS BUILDS VOCABULARY

Read-alouds expand students' vocabulary and improve their comprehension. Secondary reading requirements in content area classes are vocabulary rich. This is good—bring on new learning! All that new vocabulary, though, can be a battle for struggling readers. They might actually have a word in their auditory or oral vocabulary but do not recognize it in their reading—leading to confusion. If they hear their teacher read a passage out loud as they follow along, they can then connect a word on the page like "photosynthesis" to the word they know when listening and speaking but were unable to read it.

Just the sheer volume of words heard in context can build their vocabulary as mentioned in the previous chapter on vocabulary. Vocabulary must be taught with focus and deliberation.

READING ALOUD TO OLDER STUDENTS INCREASES FLUENCY

"When students hear frequent read-alouds, especially if they can follow the reading with a copy of the text, they learn context, pacing, inflection, pronunciation, the sheer beauty of language. They learn to visualize the story, to 'play the movie in their minds.' They begin to sense the power behind language, used and expressed purposefully, cogently, and correctly" (Punsalan, 2006).

Tips for Reading Aloud

- Use your voice to develop characters. An excited character might be talking quickly; a sad character might be talking slowly.
- When reading aloud, you can slow it down to really build the suspense—and then tell the students, "That feeling you have right now, that wanting to know more—that is suspense."
- When reading nonfiction aloud, you can model reading content area text. You can emphasize, for example, a cause and effect relationship.
- For a little teacher fun, stop reading for the day at a really suspenseful part in the book. They go crazy! It will bring reading joy to your teacher heart.
- Model the value of reading the captions for pictures—you can't just skip them—the author put important information there to help you understand.
- Display your love and excitement for the content. As Trelease asserts, your students can "sample the delights" and see your content as "pleasureful." Isn't that what we want? We want them to learn it, but don't we also want them to love it as much as we do?
- Preview the book—at least be ahead of where the kids are.
  - You'll be able to read more fluently. For example—it's easier and more effective if you know that the character is mad, so you should use a mad voice. Also, there may be a word or two you're not sure how to pronounce; look those up so that you can read them aloud fluently.
  - This will prevent any Rated R moments to accidently show up in your classroom. Sometimes it's possible to change things a little and skim by something you don't feel comfortable reading aloud, but sometimes if it is central to the plot, it doesn't really work to skip or change something.
  - You'll be able to spot and use good "think aloud" sections. For example—you can pretend to be confused about something and then "think it out" in front of the class.
  - You'll be able to secretly teach strategies. For example—if you know that something you're reading today foreshadows something happening later in the book,

you can casually make sure they notice it and when the event happens, you can say, "Oh yeah—remember when something, something, something? So *that's* why. It makes sense now."

- Introduce the book. We usually read the back of the book and the inside flaps and tell students that's what we do in real life to pick out a book. Activate any background knowledge if it seems necessary. Before reading *The Watsons Go to Birmingham—1963* by Christopher Paul Curtis aloud, give a little information about the time period and the fight for civil rights. When necessary, Lisa has her students "take a field trip to the map" to point out where the story takes place. It's important they understand the setting for Jack London's "To Build a Fire." Also, Lisa usually covers the front cover with Post-its—especially if the main character is depicted on it. She tells them it's because she wants them to visualize the character in their heads by taking the information the author gives us and imagining what he or she looks like. The picture in your head *is* how the character looks. The picture on the cover is just what some editor or graphic designer thinks they look like. The author wants you to make your own image. It's always fun to have the big reveal when the book is over. In fact, one year when Lisa read *The Outsiders* by S. E. Hinton and then showed the movie, a girl burst out and pointed at the screen and said loudly, "*That's* not what he looks like!" when the actor who played Ponyboy came on at the beginning. She had such a strong image that it shocked her to see "someone else."

- Lisa reads for the first ten minutes of class, but it works better for her neighbor next door to read during the last ten minutes. If students love the book, you can read for the first ten minutes and then bribe them by agreeing to read again at the end of class if they work really hard and get XYZ done.

- Start each read-aloud session by asking what happened in the book yesterday. It warms up their brains, puts them back into the story, and gets them ready to continue listening.

- Be careful to read at an appropriate rate. If you're nervous or uncomfortable, you might read too fast. Consciously slow down so your students have time to visualize, question, wonder, enjoy, and think.

- Read enthusiastically! Really get into it! Use different "voices" for the characters, get loud when the story calls for it, use your body language to help indicate a really sad part, if the character has an Irish brogue and you can pull it off—do it! Your students will love it. In Theodore Taylor's *The Cay*, Timothy's West Indian accent is written phonetically. Lisa shows that to the students and explains that she'll be reading aloud using that accent. At first it's a little awkward, but then everyone gets into it.

- Occasionally stop in the middle of reading and ask your students questions about the book. "Why do you think he did that? What do you think is behind that door? Has anything like this ever happened to you?" Don't make it school-y, just have a brief conversation sometimes when it's appropriate.

- Occasionally look something up during the middle of the book. *All the Earth Thrown to the Sky* by Joe R. Lansdale takes place during the Great Depression in the Dust Bowl of Oklahoma. The kids and their families in the story face devastating dust storms and the students have a hard time visualizing the magnitude of the

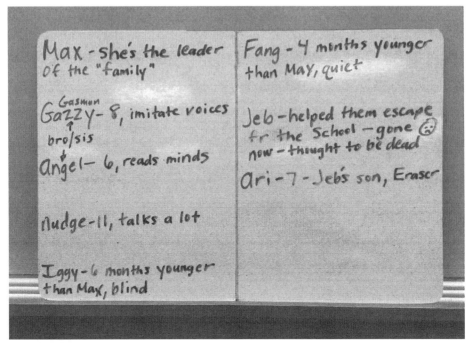

Figure 6.2. Sample character chart for *Maximum Ride: The Angel Experiment* by James Patterson. Nothing fancy. This is just displayed on the chalk tray during the read-aloud and added to when appropriate.

phenomenon. Looking up "dust storms 1930" in front of the students models intellectual curiosity as well as research skills.

- If the students need it, you can keep a chart of the characters and their traits.
- Keep an eye on your students' body language. If they start fidgeting or looking at the clock, it's time for you to stop reading (or possibly pick a new book!). We usually read for ten minutes every day. At the beginning of the year, we start with five minutes and work up to ten. We tell them that listening is a skill and they're probably rusty. We also tell them that we're rusty at reading aloud, but we'll all practice and be fine. Lisa has had classes that can listen for the whole forty-three minutes toward the end of the year when they're trying to finish a book.
- Make sure there is time after reading aloud for a brief discussion. This is a good place to ask for predictions or discuss a character's motivation.

The following section lists suggested texts that are excellent for reading aloud to students.

The lists are not meant to imply that these are the only good read-aloud children's books or series. The lists are just ten samples of books that have been successful read-alouds.

Reading Lists

CHILDREN'S BOOKS

1. *Pink and Say* by Patricia Polacco—Civil War
2. *The Wall* by Eve Bunting—Vietnam War
3. *One Grain of Rice* by Demi—exponential growth
4. *The Right Word: Roget and His Thesaurus* by Jen Bryan
5. *Trombone Shorty* by Troy Andrews—biography
6. *Martin's Big Words: The Life of Dr. Martin Luther King, Jr.* by Doreen Rappaport
7. *Science Verse* by Jon Scieszka and Lane Smith—poems about science
8. *Rose Blanche* by Roberto Innocenti—Holocoust
9. *Wilfrid Gordon McDonald Partridge* by Mem Fox—use as a writing prompt (your warm, long ago...)
10. *Snowflake Bently* by Jacqueline Briggs Martin—biography of Wilson Bently, snowflake photographer

SERIES

1. *The Maximum Ride Series* by James Patterson
2. *The Alex Rider Series* by Anthony Horowitz
3. *The Ascendance Trilogy* by Jennifer A. Nielson
4. *The Maze Runner Series* by James Dashner
5. *The Divergent Series* by Veronica Roth
6. *The Uglies* Series by Scott Westerfeld
7. *The Percy Jackson and the Olympians Series* by Rick Riordan
8. *The Matched Series* by Allie Conde
9. *The Selection Series* by Kiera Cass
10. *The Hunger Games Series* by Suzanne Collins

Why We Read Aloud

The benefits of reading aloud to older students are many. There are academic benefits and they are important, but what will keep you taking the time to read aloud is the look on your students' faces as they celebrate or laugh with a character, feel a character's love, happiness, sense of achievement, or vindication. Their faces will keep you reading aloud when you see them get angry for a character, feel a character's pain or righteous indignation. You'll keep taking the time to read aloud when you overhear students having rich discussions—without you!—about the book. It'll feel totally worth it when you see students who normally don't read on their own time, carry around a book. Mission accomplished.

References

Anderson, R. C., Hiebert, E. H., Scott, J. A., Wilkinson, I. A. G., and the Commission on Reading. (1985). *Becoming a nation of readers: The report of the Commission on Reading.* Washington, DC: National Institute of Education.

Collins, S. (2010). *Hunger Games.* New York: Scholastic.

Guignon, A. (2016, November 22). Reading aloud: Are students ever too old? *Education World.* Retrieved from http://www.educationworld.com/a_curr/curr081.shtml.

Hiebert, E. H. (2013, August 23). *Why becoming a nation of readers is still relevant.* TextProject. Retrieved from http://textproject.org/library/frankly-freddy/why-becoming-a-nation-of-readers-is-still-relevant/.

Hinds, J. D. (2015, November 25). A curriculum staple: Reading aloud to teens. *School Library Journal.* Retrieved from http://www.slj.com/2015/11/teens-ya/a-curriculum-staple-reading-aloud-to-teens/.

Korbey, H. (2013, May 14). The importance of reading aloud to older children. *Mind/Shift How We Will Learn.* Retrieved from https://ww2.kqed.org/mindshift/2013/05/14/why-reading-aloud-to-older-children-is-valuable.

Matthiessen, C. (2016, January 14). The hidden benefits of reading aloud—even for older kids. *GreatSchools.* Retrieved from http://www.greatschools.org/gk/articles/read-aloud-to-children/.

Nathional Reading Panel. (2000). *Teaching children to read.* Washington, DC: National Reading Panel.

Polacco, P. (1994). *Pink and Say.* New York: Philomel Books.

Punsalan, M. W. (2006, September). Fluency in the high school classroom: One teacher's method. *Adolescent Literacy in Perspective.*

Sachar, L. (1998). *Holes.* New York: Random House.

Scieszka, J., and Smith, L. (2004). *Science Verse.* New York: Viking Press.

Serafini, F., and Giorgis, C. (2003). *Reading aloud and beyond: Fostering the intellectual life with older readers.* Portsmouth, NH: Heinemann.

Taylor, M. The importance of reading aloud to big kids. *Brightly.* Retrieved from http://www.readbrightly.com/importance-of-reading-aloud-to-big-kids.

Trelease, J. (2013). *The read-aloud handbook* (7th ed.). New York: Penguin.

Trelease, J. (2017, January 22). *Jim Trelease's book lists.* Retrieved from Trelease-on Reading. com, http://www.trelease-on-reading.com.

Younger, S. (2013, March 6). 7 reasons why reading aloud to older kids is still very important. *Chicago Now: Between Us Parents.* Retrieved from http://www.chicagonow.com/between-us-parents/2013/03/reasons-why-reading-aloud-older-kids-tweensl-very-important/.

Zehr, M. A. (2010, January 4). *Reading aloud to teens gains favor among teachers. Education Week.* www.edweek.org/ew/articles/2010/01/06/16read_ep.h29.html.

CHAPTER 7

Writing about Reading

We often hear from teacher colleagues that their students hate to write. They are not interested in using writing as a tool to demonstrate what they know and understand. Much of their dislike about writing stems from negative experiences, and quite simply, not enough practice or encouragement to write. Writing is about developing personal voice and it also leads to greater understanding. It is no wonder that our students who struggle with reading also struggle with writing.

The connection between reading comprehension and writing was established in the last three or so decades. When students are able to express what they know and understand, it can lead to deeper and expansive thinking. James Britton (1983), one of the foundational researchers in this era, is most associated with the Writing to Learn movement. Through his research, we developed a greater understanding of the connections between writing and reading comprehension.

Arguably, our students in this digital age encounter more text-based sources than ever before. In a given day, our students send texts, post on social media, and read text on the internet. We have to admit that we too read more text now, as a result of the digital age, than we did (several decades ago) as teenagers. Our twenty-first-century students are writing today more than ever. They are writing in contexts different from what we could ever have imagined. Writing leads to learning, comprehension, and an even greater ability to express what we know and understand about our world.

In the last thirty or so years, we have benefitted from writing gurus such as Lucy Calkins, Don Murray, Tom Romano, and George Hillocks. A key paradigmatic shift in writing occurred over thirty years ago. The work of these experts, and many others, has established that students develop writing skills when they

- Write often,
- Rethink and revise their writing,
- Talk about their writing,
- Work together as a community of writers, and
- Recognize the importance of expressing what they
  know and understand through writing.

These writing tenants are reflected in the college and career readiness standards. Even more importantly, we know that when students develop their writing skills, with these writing tenants as a foundation, they achieve at higher levels and their skills in reading and developing content knowledge markedly improve.

As we dive into different writing strategies and activities that build literacy skills and content knowledge, we need to examine the writing process and its role in developing reading comprehension.

How Does the Writing Process Impact Reading Comprehension?

We generally characterize writing as the ability to compose and create text to effectively convey ideas and thinking for a variety of purposes and audiences. As a tool for communication, writing is also a tool for learning that allows our students to document their thinking, collect information, and share detailed information about what they know and understand. Additionally, writing is a tool for student self-expression and persuasion. Not only is writing a method for communication and expression, it is a tremendous learning tool. Researchers have also found that student writing skills, like reading, improves the capacity to learn (National Institute for Literacy, 2007).

As we discuss the writing process and its impact on reading comprehension, we want to make sure that we clarify the components. For several decades we've known that students develop effective writing skills that clearly articulate and communicate their thinking through a *process*. Prior to the 1980s, most writing instruction was not taught through process. Today, writing instruction is characterized as a process, rather than a product. It takes planning, revising, and reflection to craft effective writing. Today, educators generally share the following writing process model:

PREWRITING/BRAINSTORMING

During the first stage of writing, we consider topics and ideas for writing. We also think about structures that are best suited for conveying ideas and information. Should I write an essay, a poem, or a journal? The specific structure that we choose will impact our overall purpose and message.

DRAFTING

Once we consider how and what we plan to write about, it's time to write a rough draft. In the rough draft, we begin to craft and create our writing. It isn't a finished piece at this point since it is our first attempt to put our thinking into text.

REVISION AND EDITING

There is a difference between revising and editing. During revision, we reflect and consider our rough draft to ensure that our ideas and thinking are conveyed accurately. Sometimes we may need to rearrange paragraphs, rewrite sentences, delete text, or add text to our rough draft to clarify our intended message.

Editing focuses on the mechanics of writing. During the editing phase, we check grammar, punctuation, and capitalization. If a paper is riddled with mechanical errors, it can break down the meaning of text. Struggling readers often need significant support during this phase in the writing process.

PUBLISH

For most students this is when they share their writing with their teacher. When we publish our writing, we are saying, "OK, I am done and I am ready to share!"

Being able to write well is an important academic and life skill. Students who are not effective writers are denied of a critical communication and learning tool. In addition, content area teachers rely heavily on writing as a means to assess the content knowledge and comprehension of students.

Reading comprehension and writing are deeply connected. Both require students to actively create meaning and understanding. Struggling readers, as well as proficient ones, benefit from systematic writing instruction alongside reading instruction. Effective systematic writing instruction should include the following:

- Writing should be a regular part of instruction across all content areas. Like reading, the more students write, the more skilled and confident they become.
- Students need opportunities to revise work and develop ideas in extended writing activities.
- It is evident that students need literacy models for reading and writing as they develop their skills. Model writing for students and remember that it's OK if the students' writing looks like yours when they initially write. This is part of the process. Students need to imitate models for writing as they continue to hone and develop their writing skills. At some point, their individual voice and writing style will begin to emerge.
- Make writing real. Encourage students to write about topics that they care about (Hillocks, 2011).
- Display student writing in the classroom.
- Provide constructive and generative feedback about student writing. Using rubrics supports this process. If you are able to do it, avoid assigning letter or numerical grades to students. Writing is a skill that develops with practice and time. Grades are often discouraging and frequently send a negative message to students.

When students are given these opportunities in class, they are more likely to develop as writers and thinkers.

Classroom Strategies and Activities to Promote Writing Skills with Struggling Readers

Throughout our book, we wanted to provide many strategies that we have used in classrooms that are grounded in research and positive experiences with students. In this section, we will feature many "Reading to Learn" strategies and provide a strong focus on developing writing in evidence based argumentation. We will begin with argumentation.

EVIDENCE BASED ARGUMENTATION

With the promotion of college and career readiness standards, whether your state is using Common Core State Standards or its own standards, the importance of evidence based argumentation is prominent. We know that students who develop skills in evidence based argumentation become more college and career ready. They also develop their skills in reading comprehension as they create text-supported arguments. Teachers of struggling readers often ask us, "How do I get started if my students are challenged with just reading texts?" George Hillocks (2011), one of our most important literacy educators, offers some advice and guidance.

Let's remember that writing is a thinking process. Before students put pen to paper or fingers to keyboard, they need the opportunity to think. They need to learn how to support a claim, assertion, idea, or thesis with details. Hillocks suggests using visuals for students to examine and to develop this kind of thinking. As the students observe, they can make a claim about the visual and draw evidence. The following activity uses a painting from Pablo Picasso. Katie has used this activity many times in classrooms.

Step One: I begin by covering the bottom third of the painting, so that the dress is not visible. Then I tell the students that I can make several claims about this painting. For our purposes, I will offer two claims.

Claim One: The artist is depicting a human being in this painting.

Claim Two: The artist is depicting a horse.

Step Two: Instruct the students that they are going to be assigned one of the two claims and that they must find evidence from the painting to support their claim.

Step Three: At this point Katie assigns the students one of the two claims and the students discuss and analyze the painting for evidence that will support their assigned claim. From her experience, the students usually share painting details like those in chart 7.1.

This kind of activity creates interest and enthusiasm. We want students to develop their thinking first before they write. When students discuss their ideas, it leads to greater understanding and comprehension, too.

Figure 7.1. *Woman's Head* by Pablo Picasso. Printed with permission of Picasso Administration.

Claim one: The artist is depicting a human being.	Claim two: The artist is depicting a horse.
. There are two eyes. . The teeth look like they belong to a human being. . The figure has two ears. . It doesn't look like the figure has hair. . The figure has exposed skin. . The figure has eyebrows.	. There is a long black section that looks like a horse's tail (to the left of the painting). . There is a nose that looks like the narrow head and nose of a horse. . There are two eyes and ears, like a horse. . The ears are pointed like a horse.

Chart 7.1

There are many resources for visuals that can be used for this activity: paintings, photos, diagrams, maps, and videos. In our digital age, there are many resources for this activity where students can develop their ability to support a claim with evidence.

One of our favorite models for teaching evidence based argumentation is the ThinkCERCA model. Eileen Murphy, a former English teacher, created an online platform for students to develop close reading skills and evidence based writing. The CERCA model is an elegantly simplified framework than can be used for many writing contexts. It can be used for a reading journal, extended response, research paper, science lab report, editorial, debate, or the familiar academic essay.

The CERCA model stands for Claim, Evidence, Reasoning, Counterargument, Audience (and Appropriate language).

C = CLAIM   A claim is the assertion, the opinion, or thesis.

E = EVIDENCE   The proof that is needed to prove or disprove a claim. There are many places to find evidence: written text, visual media, maps, graphs, science lab data, and so on.

R = REASONING   How the writer *connects* the evidence to the claim. Reasoning is where the greatest demand on critical thinking comes into play.

C = COUNTERARGUMENT   The opportunity to address an opposing opinion or claim. In order to make an even stronger argument, address the opposing view.

A = AUDIENCE (and APPROPRIATE LANGUAGE)   Writers are better able to connect with their audience and more strongly persuade them when they are able to use language that is best suited for a particular context.

Many resources are available on the ThinkCERCA website for activities, lessons, and resources that develop close reading and evidence based argumentation skills.

There is significant research to support the evidence based argumentation and reading connection (Hillocks, 2011; Graham and Perin, 2007a and 2007b). As students work more deeply in a text, they are required to reflect and consider the deeper meanings of the text. As the students develop CERCA-like arguments, their search for evidence that supports a claim creates a context in which students have to read and reread to ensure that they comprehend the deeper meaning of a text. This is evidence that students are truly learning.

Building Comprehension and Understanding with Evidence Based Argumentation

In addition to visuals and the ThinkCERCA model, there are other learning activities that can promote reading comprehension and writing skills. Here are some more ideas.

READING JOURNALS

Prompt students to develop an opinion about a character and find evidence to support their assertion. For example, "Scout from *To Kill a Mockingbird* is a reliable narrator."

The students could list evidence from the text (using a graphic organizer is a helpful tool) for prewriting and then draft a paragraph or longer text that more clearly develops and articulates the student's claim.

STORY TRAILS

Prompt students to select three events that they thought were most important from their reading. Have the students visually depict the events and then explain *why* the event is significant.

Writing to Learn

As we previously indicated, the more students read and write, the more skilled they become. Prompted by the work of James Britton, whose research provided evidence that thinking is developed through writing, this notion is no longer revolutionary. There are many writing to learn activities that develop thinking, comprehension, and writing skills. The next section of this chapter provides many examples with specific suggestions, advice, and adaptations for struggling readers. For every activity, be sure to model the activity and your thinking. Modeling is a highly effective instructional practice for the development of reading and writing skills.

Struggling readers often do not have a voice in their head when they are reading. They can decode but when we ask them to tell us about the text, they are unable to respond. When struggling readers read a text, they don't have a voice in their head or see pictures. They aren't working toward comprehension. In working with older struggling readers, I tell them that they need to develop and listen to the voice in their head. The following strategies prompt students to listen and record the voice in their head when they are reading. These writing to learn strategies also provide students with the opportunity to practice active reading.

STICKY NOTES

When I introduce the Sticky Note strategy to students, I have a text projected. Before I read aloud the text, I say,

> *When I read a text, I have a voice in my head while I read. As I am reading, the voice in my head might ask a question about the text, make a comment, or I might have a personal connection. As I read aloud the text to you, every time I have a question, comment, or connection about the text, I am going to write it down on a sticky note.*

At this point, I read the text that's projected and every time I have a comment, question, or connection, I write it down on a sticky note and place it in the text where I stopped.

This demonstration can be an effective mini-lesson.

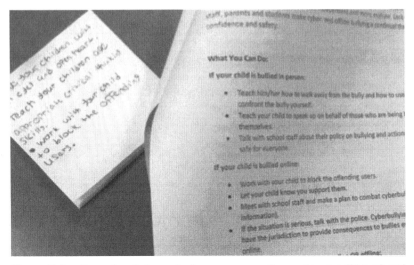

Figure 7.2.   Sample sticky note from a seventh grader reading about bullying.

STOP AND WRITE

In the Stop and Write activity, students are instructed to stop at certain points in the text to fill in the following chart. The chart can be used in a notebook, on a word processing document, or given to the students as a graphic organizer. The chart has two columns. The first column, titled "What I know," prompts students to recall basic information about the text. By the way, the mere recall of information from a text is the lowest level of comprehension. The second column, titled "What I am thinking," prompts students to question, comment, and make predictions about the text. Here's a tip, if the reader's second column,

What I know	What I am thinking
The story takes place in Alabama. It's a long time ago. It takes place during the Depression and there are some kids in the story. The kids are Scout and Jem. They are brother and sister. Their dad is Atticus and he's a lawyer.	I am thinking that people during the Depression were poor and not happy most of the time. It reminds me of a couple of years ago when people were losing their homes in my neighborhood because they lost their jobs. I wonder what happened to Scout and Jem's mom. I want to know why the summer changed Scout's life.

Chart 7.2

"What I am thinking," looks identical to the first one and contains a mere recollection of facts and information from the text, then there are some breakdowns in comprehension. When readers question, comment, and make predictions about the text, there's some high level comprehension occurring. Model and demonstrate the strategy for the students. Here's a sample Stop and Write using *To Kill a Mockingbird*.

READING JOURNALS

Like other Writing to Learn strategies, Reading Journals are an opportunity to explore thinking through writing. It's a vehicle for students to record their thinking. There are many strategies and ways to approach a reading journal with your students. With struggling readers, it is often helpful to provide structure for the students. We like to add a vocabulary section with our students.

Vocabulary Section/Personal Dictionary

Students record words that they encounter in their reading that they may have seen but aren't sure of the meaning and words they don't recognize and have never seen before. Chart 7.3 provides a helpful structure for students to record their words.

Students could use this vocabulary chart along with the Stop and Write strategy in their reading journal. The Stop and Write helps students to focus and explore a text.

I WAS THERE

Creative dramatic games provide a kinesthetic pathway for students to express what they know and understand about a text. Drawing from the old radio show *I Was There*, students summarize and retell a text as if they were present. Once the students verbally retell the text-based story, they are prompted to draft a written version. We suggest the following steps.

Word	Page # and sentence that contains the word	Synonym	Antonym	Illustration of the word

Chart 7.3. Sample vocabulary chart.

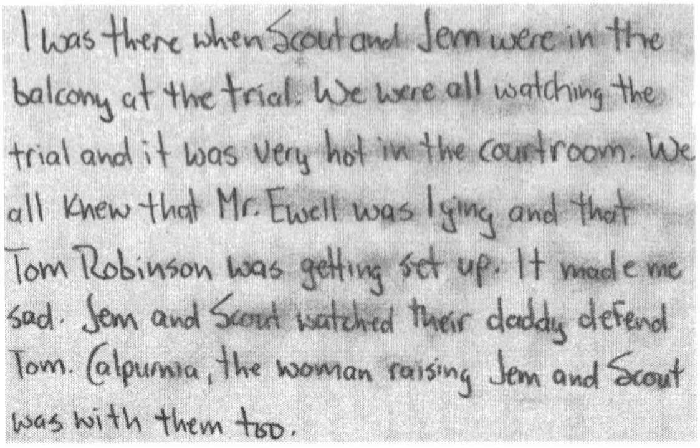

I was there when Scout and Jem were in the balcony at the trial. We were all watching the trial and it was very hot in the courtroom. We all knew that Mr. Ewell was lying and that Tom Robinson was getting set up. It made me sad. Jem and Scout watched their daddy defend Tom. Calpurnia, the woman raising Jem and Scout was with them too.

Figure 7.3

We usually divide the students into groups of four to five for this activity. In the groups, prompt the students to pretend as if they were present in the story, and like a reporter, they are going to summarize and retell the story. They practice with their peers in the small groups; then either individually or as a small group, the students create a written version of the summarization or retelling. It is important to model this activity for the students prior to having them work independently. See the sample in figure 7.3.

From this student sample, you can see that the reader is mostly retelling the facts about this scene from *To Kill a Mockingbird.* When student responses are composed mostly of the retelling of information and facts, they are generally in a basic mode of comprehension on a text. When students begin to ask questions and make comments about the text, they are deepening and broadening their comprehension. Figure 7.4 shows what that might look like.

In this student sample, the student ponders Tom's innocence, and the lying Ewells. The student is also making inferences about the climate and the context of the scene. When students begin to ask these kinds of questions, they are becoming more active readers and deepening their comprehension.

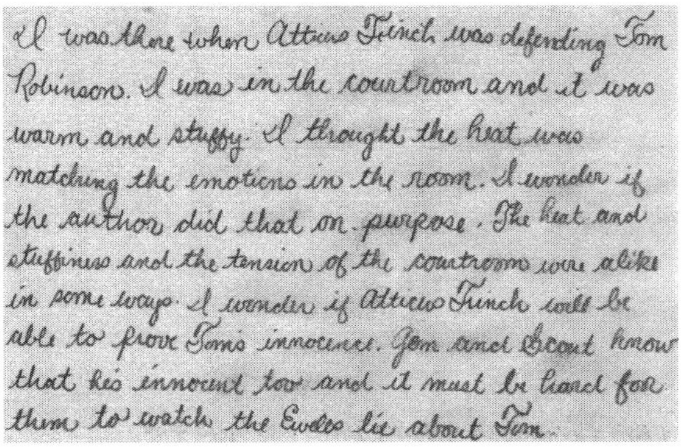

I was there when Atticus Finch was defending Tom Robinson. I was in the courtroom and it was warm and stuffy. I thought the heat was matching the emotions in the room. I wonder if the author did that on purpose. The heat and stuffiness and the tension of the courtroom were alike in some ways. I wonder if Atticus Finch will be able to prove Tom's innocence. Jem and Scout know that he's innocent too and it must be hard for them to watch the Ewells lie about Tom.

Figure 7.4

In this passage, _____ (insert character's name) is

_____ (describe what the character does).

I think the character is _____

_____ (write down your opinion of the character).

Other characters in the story feel _____

_____ (insert how the other characters react) about

_____ (insert character's name).

Figure 7.5. Sample sentence stems, also known as structured prompts.

CHARACTER BIOGRAPHY

 Character biographies are a great strategy for students to learn about point of view for both fictional and informational texts. As students explore point of view and characterization, they should consider questions like

- How does the passage make you react to, or think about characters or events within the narrative?
- Are there colors, sounds, or physical descriptions that appeal to the senses and help the reader to understand the character?
- Who speaks in the passage? To whom does he or she speak? Does the narrator have a limited or partial point of view?

In this activity, the students select a character to follow throughout the text. The students record information about the character that could be in response to the previous questions. You could also use sentence stems (sentence stems are structured prompts) like those in figure 7.5.

In general, sentence stems are more structured and a helpful tool for our most struggling readers. Modeling and providing a structure helps students delve into the text and begin to analyze text elements.

Conclusion

When students can express what they know and understand about the texts they read through their writing, they have reached the level of comprehension that is characteristic of competent, independent, and fluent readers. To reach this level of proficiency, students need ample opportunities to write about the texts they read. Developing this greater level of comprehension and parallel writing skills will deepen a student's understanding. Students do not have to receive a formal grade for every writing assignment. Encourage student to write as a means to develop greater understanding and to express what they know and understand about a topic from their reading.

References

Applebee, A., and Langer, J. (2006). *The state of writing instruction: What does existing data tell us.* Albany, NY: Center on English Learning and Achievement.

Biancarosa, G., and Snow, C. (2004). *Reading next—A vision for action and research in middle and high school literacy: A report to Carnegie Corporation of New York.* Washington, DC: Alliance for Excellence in Education.

Britton, J. (1983). Language and learning across the curriculum. *Essays on Theory and Practice in the Teaching of Writing.* Upper Montclair, NJ: Boynton/Cook.

Eunice Kennedy Shriver National Institute of Child Health and Human Development, NIH, DHHS. (2010). Adapted from *What Content-Area Teachers Should Know About Adolescent Literacy* (NA). Retrieved from https://www.nichd.nih.gov/publications/Pages/pubs_details.aspx?pubs_id=5752.

Graham, S., and Perin, D. (2007a). *Writing next: Effective strategies to improve writing of adolescents in middle and high schools.* New York: Carnegie Corporation of New York.

Graham, S., and Perin, D. (2007b). A meta-analysis of writing instruction for adolescent students. *Journal of Educational Psychology, 99,* 445–476.

Hillocks, G. (2011). *Teaching argument writing, grades 6–12: Supporting claims with relevant evidence and clear reasoning.* Portsmouth, NH: Heinemann.

Kiewra, K. (1989). A review of note-taking: The encoding-storage paradigm and beyond. *Educational Psychology Review, 1,* 147–174.

Kiuhara, S., Graham, S., and Hawken, L. (2009).Teaching writing to high school students: A national survey. *Journal of Educational Psychology, 101,* 136–160.

Langer, J., and Applebee, A. (1987). *How writing shapes thinking: A study of teaching and learning.* Urbana, IL: National Council of Teachers of English.

Nelson, N., and Calfee, R. (1998).The reading-writing connection. In N. Nelson and R. Calfee (Eds.), *Ninety-seventh yearbook of the National Society for the Study of Education* (Part II, pp. 1–52). Chicago, IL: National Society for the Study of Education.

Scammacca, N., Roberts, G., Vaughn, S., Edmonds, M., Wexler, J., Reutebuch, C., and Torgesen, J. (2007). *Intervention for struggling readers: A meta-analysis with implications for practice.* Portsmouth, NH: RMC Research Corp.

Slavin, R., Cheung, A., Groff, C., and Lake, C. (2008). Effective reading programs for middle and high schools: A best evidence synthesis. *Reading Research Quarterly, 43,* 290–322.

Stotsky, S. (1982).The role of writing in developmental reading. *Journal of Reading, 31,* 320–340.

Part Three

CLASSROOM MANAGEMENT

CHAPTER 8

Running Records to Assess Reading

INSTRUCTIONAL MAPS

As students develop their reading skills, it's important to individually monitor progress. Preschool and primary teachers often track student development of reading skill development with "running records." Keeping individual running records is important since it monitors what skills students are mastering and which ones need greater attention and development. For adolescent readers who struggle and need to master basic reading skills, running records can also foster a growth mind-set instead of a deficit mind-set.

Lisa and Katie have encountered many students at the middle and high school level who have experienced negative reading experiences. They consistently receive messages that they don't read well and this becomes a self-fulfilling prophecy. Students think, "All of the teachers and adults think I am a lousy reader, so I must be." Richard Cash discusses this in greater depth in chapter 10. Like other academic skills, reading develops when skills are developed through positive contexts and a growth mind-set (Cash, 2016). Running records monitor student skill development through a growth model, not a punitive or deficit structure. Thus, students develop a more positive experience and are more willing to work at what has been historically difficult for them.

Why Do We Need Running Records?

We've all had students in our class who struggle with reading. Most secondary level teachers—including English teachers—have little to no training in how to teach reading, but we see our students struggle and would like to help. We love our content and we want our students to love it too! Yet it is frustrating when we realize that there are students in our classes who can't access the content via the assigned reading. When we add that frustration to not really knowing how to help, it can be discouraging for a teacher. A running record can help.

A running record is a quick assessment of how a student reads continuous text. There are different components and layers in the reading process. The first two parts of this book focus on two major components—the ability to decode and the ability to comprehend (with fluency as the bridge between them). You've read that there are layers of decoding and layers of comprehension. A running record can help us figure out which one of those two major components causes our students to struggle. Is it decoding? Is it comprehension? Can they decode, but is it so disfluent that there is no room for comprehension? The information attained in a running record will guide us to address a specific deficit. A running record is a way for the teacher to establish what, specifically, the student struggles with so he can help them. Running records are a diagnose-and-prescribe procedure.

In addition to determining the specific struggle, a running record can also show you what, if any, strategies the reader uses to solve an unknown word (chapters 1–3). If it's an effective strategy—great! If not, you could suggest a more useful strategy. It can also inform you if the reader self-monitors and self-corrects while reading (see chapters 5 and 9). If they do—great! If not, you can talk to them about "thinking about their thinking"—metacognition, as mentioned in chapters 5 and 9. A running record could alert you to vocabulary (chapter 3) or background knowledge gaps. There are none? Great! If there are gaps, closing them could make a huge difference in accessing the content. A running record will also give you an idea about their level of reading fluency (chapter 4).

WHAT IS A RUNNING RECORD?

Lisa earned her master's in reading to be a better English teacher—not to teach reading. So when she became a reading specialist, running records were new and a little scary. Unless you specifically teach reading, there's no reason you'd be familiar with running records.

In her book *When Kids Can't Read: What Teachers Can Do*, Kylene Beers included a great example of a classroom use of a running record. In the passage, her student becomes frustrated while struggling to read "The Gift of the Magi" by O. Henry (Beers, 2003, p. 29). The student wrestles with the text, trying to sound out unfamiliar words and tease out the meaning of a simple metaphor. Eventually, he gives up and has great difficulty even being able to tell the teacher what it was about. The example is as heartbreaking as it is familiar.

This student is reading at what is called the "frustrational" level—it is above his reading level. There are three levels when we're assessing students: independent, instructional, and frustration.

- Independent Level: This is the level a student can read on his or her own without help from the teacher. Elementary teachers use a quick test for this called the "five finger test." If a student can read a passage of about a hundred words and know all but about five of the words, that is the independent level of reading. This is the place to build reading stamina and fluency.
- Instructional Level: This is the level where a student can successfully read with teacher support. The student needs to be able to read a hundred-word passage and

know all but ten of the words. This is the place where teachers can work on vocabulary and reading strategies—extending students' knowledge and comprehension.

• Frustration Level: This is the level where a student can successfully read less than 90 percent of the words in a hundred-word passage; they have difficulty with at least twenty of the words. Reading at this level (maybe for years) can cause a lot of frustration! It can also cause a lack of motivation.

It is not fair for us to expect our students to magically be able to read and understand our content when they do not have the skills. A running record can identify the skills that are lacking so we can guide our students through the content so they can actually learn it.

Running records help teachers evaluate students' reading behaviors. Reading is an invisible process, so for successful intervention to take place, it is critical that we make a struggling readers' process visible. A running record can do this.

How to Give a Running Record

To give a running record, the teacher has the student read aloud a short portion of the text. The teacher also has a copy of the text and records exactly what the student reads using a marking system to note miscues (errors) in order to inform instruction.

Figure 8.1.   Teacher giving a running record to a student.

Accurate reading	Do nothing if you have a copy of the text. If you do not have a copy of the same text, make a check mark for each correct word.
Substitution	Write the word the reader said over the word.
Insertion	Use a caret and write in the word.
Omission	Cross out the word, or word part, the reader omitted.
Repitition	Underline the word(s) or phrase(s) each time they were repeated.
Self-correction	Write *SC* after the error.
Hesitation	Mark an ellipsis (...) where the reader hesitated.
Sounded the word out	Write *SO* above the word that was sounded out.

Chart 8.1.   Modified Running Record Marking System

If your student...	Then prompt your student to...
Does not read the punctuation	Notice the punctuation. Pause at the end of a sentence, practice making your voice go down at the end of a statement and up at the end of a question.
Does not seem to notice italics, bold or colored print	Notice italics, bold or colored print. Remind reader that the by using these cues, the author is telling us it is important.
Does not seem to notice headings, pictures, captions, or side bars	Notice all of these nonfiction features. The author puts important information there to help us organize it in our heads so we can learn it.
Doesn't notice suffixes	Read to the end of the word. Is there a suffix?
Sounds out the first letter, repeats it a few times and then guesses a word with the same beginning	Look for syllables, prefixes, suffixes, base words. Break the guessing habit!
Omits or adds words	Recognize this habit. Emphasize that in order to know what the author is saying, a reader has to read the words that are there.
Substitutes words	Recognize this habit. Emphasize that in order to know what the author is saying, a reader has to read the words that are there.
Is willing to keep reading even though they just read a nonsense word (mispronounced and said a nonword)	Read it again and ask themselves, "Does that make sense?"
Is willing to keep reading even though they can tell something isn't right	Read it again and ask themselves, "Does that sound right?"
Can't tell you anything about what they read	Self-reflect about how he/she reads. Depending on the issue, you can suggest strategies discussed elsewhere in this book, for example: Tape-assisted reading, phrased reading (from Chapter 4) Sequence of events, cause and effect, point of view (from Chapter 5) Visualization, stop-and-write, sticky notes (from Chapter 7)
Reads word by word	Read in phrases or"read like talking"
Reads in a monotone voice	Read like you're talking or explaining to a friend

Chart 8.2.   If/Then Chart for Reading

Running records aren't just for use in reading class or interventions. They can also be used in content area classes. There is a commonly accepted marking system that you could easily find online. Eventually you might modify the system to fit your needs. See chart 8.1 to see a modified marking system.

It's important to resist the urge to help students or give them hints. At first that may be difficult, but eventually when you see the value in knowing exactly where they are without you, it gets easier. Sometimes they just stop and wait for help. Waiting for help might be their number one reading strategy! We have to supply them with more. After about three seconds, tell them, "It's OK for what we're doing for you to just keep going." If you think that they're pausing to decode the word in their head, ask them to please do all of their think work out loud so you can see how they read.

As soon as the student finishes reading, evaluate their level of fluency while reading. Was it mostly word by word? Were there some short phrases? Did most or all of the reading sound fluent? Did they read with expression and proper intonation or was it read in a monotone? Make a note of their level of fluency. It is common to assign them a 1 (mostly nonfluent), 2 (mostly fluent), or a 3 (reading fluently).

After they're done reading aloud, ask them some questions about what they just read to check for understanding. It could be as simple as "Tell me what this was about," like in the Kylene Beers example above. You may be shocked to find out you have students in your class who can read every word perfectly but are unable to tell you anything about it. It was just a string of words to them, so they need some reminders to "think about their thinking" and use comprehension strategies. Make a note of their comprehension level.

HOW TO CONDUCT A MISCUE ANALYSIS

After the student has read aloud and you've recorded their reading, you will conduct a miscue analysis. A miscue analysis (studying the errors) can reveal where the reading process broke down and which strategies need to be taught or practiced. Making reading visible in a running record can also determine what strategies the student successfully uses.

It might be helpful for you to construct an If/Then chart according to your content's reading needs (see Chart 8.2 as an example).

Miscue Analysis for Social Studies Example

The two issues to address for Carrie are reading the endings of words and using the text features of nonfiction. She had issues with reading punctuation and some substitutions, but you have to pick your battles.

Carrie needs to read to the end of the words and notice and read any suffixes. She also needs to notice and use the nonfiction features. She did not read the heading, or the Did You Know sidebar or the captions for the pictures. She needs to

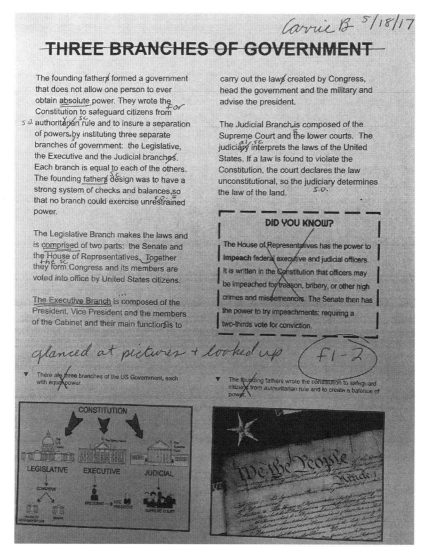

Figure 8.2. Social Studies Running Record sample. Used with permission from Nicole Verbeten.

understand that the author puts information in these locations to help the reader understand the content.

Carrie scored 2 out of 3 and would be considered to be mostly fluent. She wasn't reading word by word, choppy, or in a monotone, but she did repeat and missed punctuation.

Carrie was able to summarize accurately the portion of the text that she read and comprehends most of the text. She, obviously, couldn't say anything about the portions of the page she skipped, so that would affect her total comprehension of the text if she were assessed.

Miscue Analysis for Mathematics Example

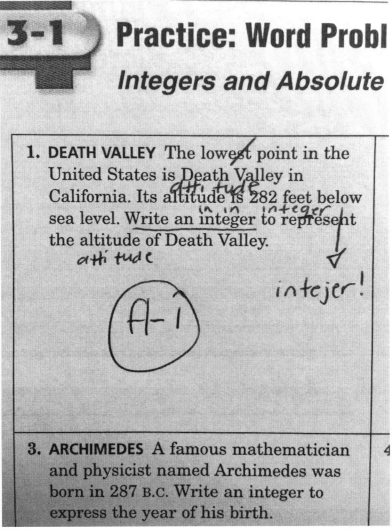

Figure 8.3. Mathematics Running Record sample from *Mathematics: Applications and Concepts, Course 2*. Reprinted with permission from Glencoe/McGraw-Hill.

This student missed a suffix, but the two things to address here are guessing a more familiar word, 'attitude,' for the actual word, 'altitude.' He probably knows what altitude means, but he might relate it to an airplane, not Death Valley and sea level. This student needs to read what's actually in the text and not guess. He probably knew something wasn't right because he paused after the first two syllables—both times, but his habit is to guess, even when it doesn't make sense and just keep going. He needs to break the guessing habit.

It looks like he had the word 'integer' in his listening vocabulary, but not his reading vocabulary. He at first started repeating the familiar syllable 'in' then went on to use a hard 'g,' but knew that wasn't right and then realized (with excitement) it was 'integer'—the word they've been talking about in math! The only thing now though is what on earth is the 'attitude' of Death Valley? How confusing. It's possible he can do the math, but because he couldn't do the reading, we may never know.

It's a little hard to judge fluency with such a short passage, but in five short lines of text he was disfluent three times so he earned a 1 out of 3. It's possible that he'd be able to read another word problem more fluently if he knew the vocabulary better.

This is an example of where a Word Wall could come in handy for secondary teachers. Our content is so vocabulary rich—we need to make sure our students are learning the words. The first day you introduce integers put the word on the unit word wall so they can connect their listening vocabulary with their reading vocabulary—and it will be there to copy for their writing vocabulary.

Conclusion

The majority of older students won't need a running record, but for students who are struggling with accessing the content, a running record could point out their deficit so the teacher can address it. It could be something as simple as pointing out the importance of nonfiction features they're skipping, or as complicated as coaching them to select which comprehension strategy they need to employ at that moment. Running records can help teachers see if the parts are working together smoothly—and if not, to guide them toward a successful reading and comprehension experience.

References

Baker, L., and Hammond, R. (2001). *Life in the deserts.* Chicago: World Book.

Beers, K. (2003). *When kids can't read: What teachers can do.* Portsmouth, NH: Heinemann.

Cash, R. M. (2016): *Self-Regulation in the classroom: Helping students learn how to learn.* Minneapolis: Free Spirit Publishing.

Fried, M. D. (2013). Activating teaching: Using running records to inform teaching decisions. *Journal of Reading Recovery, 13*(1), 5–16.

Gaskell, M. (2014). *Determining middle grades teacher perspectives on running records improving reading fluency.* (Unpublished doctoral dissertation). Northcentral University.

Teaching as Leadership. (2003). Identifying the source of reading difficulties. Retrieved from www.teachingasleadership.org, January 25, 2017.

Mathematics applications and concepts, course 2. (2004). New York: Glencoe/McGraw Hill.

McKenna, M. C., and Stahl, K. A. D. (2015). *Assessment for reading instruction.* New York: Guilford Publications.

Shea, M. (2007). Where's the glitch? How to use running records with older readers, grades 5–8. *Education Review//Reseñas Educativas.*

CHAPTER 9

Self-Regulation, Mind-Set, Motivation, and the Struggling Reader

Richard Cash[1]

In today's world, distractions abound: cell phones, the internet, constant advertising in every venue. Our students are more distracted today than at any other time in human history. These distractions can have a costly effect in the classroom. Researchers at Carnegie Mellon conducted a study designed to measure the brain-drain of disruption and found that there was a 20 percent drop in cognitive testing scores between those who were distracted versus those subjects who were focused (Sullivan, 2013). Distraction, or the inability to manage it, could account for the over 30 percent of students who fail to achieve basic reading proficiency by fourth grade and an even higher number (55 percent) for those students who attend high-poverty schools (National Assessment of Educational Progress [NAEP], 2007). These findings suggest that, in additional to early literacy skills, students who are unable to manage themselves to avoid distraction are less likely to achieve academic success.

Avoiding distractions, or the ability to differentiate competing attention, is one aspect of self-regulation for learning. Students who are aware of, use, and adjust their abilities to self-regulate are more likely to invest effort into learning. Self-regulation for learning is the balancing of affect (feelings), behaviors (actions), and cognition (thinking). Cash (2016b) names these the ABCs of learning. In the development of literacy and learning, owning, managing, and adjusting one's ABCs can have a substantial effect on achievement and well-being.

Defining Self-Regulation for Learning (SRL)

For more than four decades, the topic of self-regulation has been studied in the field of psychology. Only recently has it become evident that students who possess higher degrees of self-regulation are more likely to achieve academic goals. As noted above, the world our students inhabit is one of constant distraction. Teaching students how to manage their affect, behavior, and cognition is a critical aspect of achieving learning autonomy.

---

1. The authors would like to express their gratitude to Richard Cash for this contributing chapter.

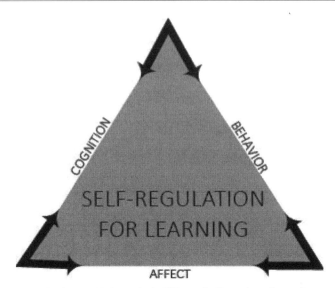

Figure 9.1. ABCs of Self-Regulation for Learning,
© Richard M. Cash, EdD. Reprinted with permission.

Barry Zimmerman, an educational researchers at City University in New York, and Dale Schunk, an education psychologist in the School of Education at the University of North Carolina, Greensboro, state that self-regulation for learning is the self-generated management of feelings, behaviors, and thoughts that assist us in attaining personal and academic goals (2001). Cash (2016b) articulates these dimensions as the ABCs (affect, behavior and cognition) of self-regulation for learning. The balancing act within the three dimensions of self-regulation are essential for achieving both academic and life success.

Richard and Katie also identified the strong connection of the ABCs for learning when they provided professional development in several school districts. With Richard's expertise in this area and Katie's in literacy, they quickly realized that there are deep connections with self-regulation and literacy development.

A = AFFECT

How students feel about a learning setting determines the focus of their attention. The terms *feelings* and *emotions* are often used synonymously, when in fact they are different from each other. Emotions are the chemical reaction within the limbic system of the midbrain (the "emotional center"). These chemical reactions are natural to our brain's processing and survival systems. These emotions signal our body and prefrontal cortex (the "thinking center") to respond. These responses are called "feelings." The physical reactions often appear as facial expressions, body movement, or modulation of voice.

This is connected to reading because it is a sociopsycholinguistic process (Smith, 2012). There are deep connections between reading success and a child's experiences. Children who are read to and grow up in homes with books and other reading materials are more likely to be successful readers. They "feel" good about reading. Conversely, when children have negative experiences with reading and feel like they have failed, they often become reluctant readers and struggle with the development of skills they need for lifelong success in reading (Conlon et al., 2006). Our students must have positive experiences with reading and this will, in turn, create a more positive affect.

B = BEHAVIOR

How students manage themselves in the classroom is considered the behavioral aspect of self-regulation. The actions students employ before, during, and after the learning do have a substantial effect on achievement. These actions include learning strategies and skills; and physical and behavioral management techniques, such as following classroom procedures. Researchers Paris and Paris (2001) found that effective teachers can promote literacy skill attainment through encouraging their students to develop self-regulated strategies. We can teach students to deliberately modulate their responses to external and internal stimuli by providing them with specific skills for persisting on academic tasks and completing work independently.

Teaching students how to organize themselves prior to, during, and after instruction is one of the many tools of behavioral self-regulation. Prior to instruction, teachers should explain the purpose of the activities, describe upcoming activities, and provide scaffolding opportunities for students to practice. Teachers, who themselves are organized, can have a tremendous effect on classroom management and student performance, especially during what is called "noninstructional time." Noninstructional time is transitional activities, moving from space to space, waiting for the teacher to begin lessons, standing in line, or waiting for the distribution of materials (Connor et al., 2010).

Behaviors and habits of reading are developed through some of our best practices in reading (Moore et al., 1999). For example,

- Giving students choices in their reading and teaching them *how* to select reading materials and books.
- Developing habits of reading. Literature circles, book clubs, reading workshops, guided reading are all pedagogies that develop students' habits and behaviors to become proficient and independent readers.

There is definitely still time to develop these behaviors and habits in adolescent readers. Katie has had numerous examples of classroom settings where when students are given choice, support, and more opportunities to read a large variety of texts, reading abilities improve dramatically. Supporting these habits leads students to read more and become better readers.

C = COGNITION

Cognition is the term used for the mental process of learning. Simple cognition is the recognition of sensory inputs, such as awareness of smells, sounds, tastes, movement, and the recall of factual information. Whereas complex cognition is the higher levels of thinking that include abstractions of thought in critical reasoning, interpretation, and creativity. The more often students are provided experiences that encourage complex thinking beyond factual retrieval the more likely they will be able to use advanced levels of thinking more fluently.

There are three levels of cognition to be considered in the classroom. Metacognition, what is commonly called the "thinking about your own thinking" level, is that which is thinking about the self. More generally, metacognition in the classroom is reflective thinking—the process of remembering what has just occurred as well as what has happened in the past. This also includes the mental actions of planning, monitoring, and evaluating performances. Metacognition is also essential to our abilities to manage our executive functioning (Cash, 2016b). Knowing your learning orientation, or the way you like to learn best, and knowing what is expected before, during, and after a task are all forms of metacognition. Effective learners know their strengths and limitations when it comes to approaching problems and tasks.

Infracognition is the broader thinking structures used daily in school. These include what are typically considered twenty-first-century skills of critical reasoning, creativity, communication, and collaboration. These tools are used when solving problems and making decisions. As noted in the Spectrum of Thinking (Cash, 2016a), the act of thinking moves between convergent to divergent thinking. Convergent thinking, logical, step by step, based in facts is useful when solving well-formed problems and situations. Divergent thinking, thinking that generates many ideas, "out of the box" thinking, connecting new and old ideas is useful when needing creative solutions to ill-formed situations or new imaginative ideas. Both are critical in the problem-solving process. A factor of cognitive self-regulation is knowing which tools of infracognition to use and when to use them.

The most advanced level of cognition is metaphysical cognition, or "thinking beyond the self." Metaphysics is a philosophical line of abstract or theoretical thinking. Analogies are a common form of metaphysical thinking, such as "In what ways is the structure of an atom similar/dissimilar to system?" (Emmet, 1949). Essential questions using the "why" format are also a component of metaphysical cognition (example: "Why do changes have positive and negative effects?"). Incorporating both types of questions into content offers students the opportunity to expand learning beyond the classroom.

As the authors of this book have reiterated, struggling readers' attention is often mired in the physical aspects of text. The opening chapters provide information and suggestions to remedy these difficulties that adolescent readers might still be struggling with. Once the students have cracked the code, comprehension and the cognition of the text becomes more accessible. In previous chapters, the authors describe many activities that nurture student comprehension of text and thinking about the text, or the metacognition. Once students are able to reach this level, they are at the cognitive level that Cash refers to.

Phases of Learning

Self-regulation for learning and literacy develop within a cycle of learning or what Cash (2016a) defines as Four Phases of Engaging in a Task (see figure 9.2). At first, a student must feel a sense of confidence to pursue the tasks required. Next, a plan for the learning needs to occur; this includes the what, where, and when of the tasks. The third phase is monitoring, adjusting when necessary, and reworking when needed. The final stage is the review and reflection stage. In the final stage the learner reviews what occurred, considers options for renewal or change, and sets a tone for the next learning task.

PHASE ONE: FOSTERING CONFIDENCE

During each of the phases of engaging in a task, specific self-regulatory aspects are employed as well as literacy strategies. Phase one is where students must focus on the right mind-set to do well. Mind-set, as defined by Dweck (2006), shifts from a fixed mind-set (intelligence and ability are a fixed trait and are unlikely to change) to

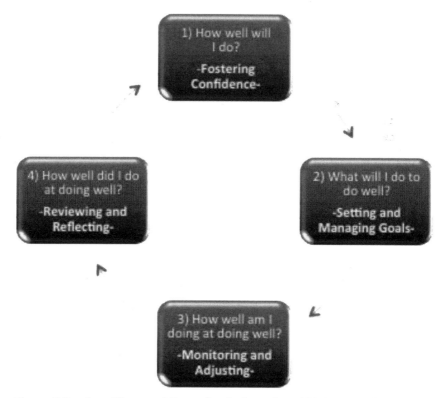

Figure 9.2.   Four Phases of Engaging in Learning, ©Richard M. Cash, EdD. Reprinted with permission.

Affect	Behavior	Cognition
• Safe & welcoming environment • Building self-esteem & confidence • Emotional resilience	• Set scholarly expectations • Develop academic habits, language • Introduce the use of content language • Actively uncover prior knowledge	• Develop questioning strategies • Build academic/ scholarly thinking • Strategies to shift mindset
Literacy Strategies Read Aloud, Graphic Organizers, KWL/KIQ, Vocabulary Engagement/Instruction, Pre-Writing, Anticipatory Activities to Increase Interest, Word Sort/Trees, Brainstorming		

Chart 9.1. © Richard M. Cash, EdD, and Katherine McKnight, PhD. Reprinted with permission.

a growth mind-set (intelligence and ability are malleable and can change with hard work and effort). We all possess both mind-sets, but what makes us successful is the ability to shift to a growth mind-set when necessary. Ensuring students have the right mind-set for the task includes providing a safe and welcoming environment where they feel confidence and that self-efficacy can grow. Students are clearly aware of the expectations, norms, and classroom procedures. Cognitively, students know particular learning strategies to assist them in the upcoming tasks (see the following charts).

Other ideas for fostering confidence in the classroom include

- Setting and maintaining acceptable learning behaviors in the classroom.
- Using a nonconfrontational style with your students—don't get into power struggles!
- Using affirmative language rather than punitive language ("Jamal is really focused on the task at hand!" rather than "Sarah, stay on task.")
- Giving students time to destress—play fun games or tell jokes after a difficult task, activity, or test.
- Refusing to engage in public arguments—don't allow students to "get your goat." If a student has a disagreement with you, take the student aside to debate or discuss it.

PHASE TWO: SETTING AND MANAGING GOALS

In phase two, students make plans and set goals for achieving success. We can assist students in maintaining their confidence to approach tasks when they find worth and value in what's to come. Piquing student interest in the content is one way to engage students in wanting to know more—thus encouraging their confidence in setting goals. Teachers must set clear goals themselves for the upcoming tasks, making sure students know what is expected and required. Students must also have the infracognitive thinking strategies readily available.

Goal setting is an excellent way to focus students on achieving academic success. Using the acronym SMART can help students set a plan of action:

Specific: focusing the target on something you want to improve upon
Measurable: being able to measure your success
Assignable: listing the steps, materials, and resources you will need to reach your goal

Affect	Behavior	Cognition
• Encourage confidence through content awareness	• Learn study behaviors	• Critical reasoning
• Manage stress, **"boredom"** & distractions	• Develop organizational skills	• Essential question development & use
• Maintain a safe/risk-free environment	• Maintain high expectations	• Creative thinking
	• Teach goal setting	• HOTS
	• Learn how to ask for help	
	• Learn to avoid distraction	
	• Strategies to overcome helplessness	
Literacy Strategies		
KWL/KIQ, Peer Assisted-Learning Strategies (PALS), Directed Reading and Thinking Activities (DRTA), Reader Response Journals, Note Taking Systems (Cornell), Structured Note Taking, Organizational Strategies, Graphic Organizers, Question Prompts, Concept Mapping, Brainstorming, Vocabulary Mapping, Formative Process		

Chart 9.2. © Richard M. Cash, EdD, and Katherine McKnight, PhD. Reprinted with permission.

Relevant: making sure that the goal is within your reach with the resources you have
Time-bound: setting a time line for reaching your goal

PHASE THREE: MONITORING AND ADJUSTING

A critical aspect of learning is the ability to recognize when strategies are working and when they are not. The monitoring and adjusting phase of learning requires that students are fully aware of their own progress in learning. This is most often done through the use of formative assessment strategies. Qualify formative assessment is descriptive in nature and tells students what they are doing when and where they may need to adjust and rework. Descriptive feedback must be

• Ongoing throughout the learning process,
• Provided to the learning in a timely manner,

Affect	Behavior	Cognition
• Maintain confidence through success awareness	• Use & monitor study behaviors	• Routinely using thinking tools
• Manage stress, "boredom" & distractions	• Use & monitor organizational skills	• Constructing essential questions and HOT questions
• Maintain a safe/risk-free environment	• Maintain high expectations	• Implement creativity
	• Monitor goal approach	
	• Monitor assistance seeking	
	• Monitor distractions	
Literacy Strategies		
Pre-assessment, Formative Process including Descriptive Feedback, Anticipation Guides, Entrance/ Exit Slips, Question/Answer Relationships (QAR), Questioning the Author, Selective Highlighting, Marking Up the Text/Annotation, Reciprocal Teaching, Writing to Learn, Jigsaw, Frayer Model, Stop & Jot, Growth Mindset Questions		

Chart 9.3. © Richard M. Cash, EdD, and Katherine McKnight, PhD. Reprinted with permission.

Affect	Behavior	Cognition
• Assess confidence through successes	• Assess study behaviors	• Reflection through meta-cognition
• Assess stress, "boredom" & distractions levels	• Assess organizational skills	• Forecast mindset into the future
• Suggest environmental adaptations/adjustments	• Assess meeting expectations	
	• Assess goal attainment	

Literacy Strategies

Summative Assessment Process, Reflection Logs, Portfolio Development, Collaborative Student Conversation, Teacher/Student Coaching Session, Summarizing (GIST),   Graphic Representations of Learning, Goal Charting, Growth Mindset Compliments

Chart 9.4. © Richard M. Cash, EdD, and Katherine McKnight, PhD. Reprinted with permission.

- Explicitly focused on skill and self-regulatory development,
- Specific to the goals, tasks, and performances,
- Incremental (neither too much nor too little), and
- Effort focused rather than achievement focused.

PHASE FOUR: REVIEWING AND REFLECTING

The final stage is the reflective stage. Students must take time to identify what worked, why it work, what didn't work, why it didn't work, and what to do next time. Often, summative assessments can help students identify how close to the learning goals they achieved, as well as document effective use of strategies. During this phase metacognition must be prompted by the teacher to help students develop greater SRL. Taking time to process and reflect before the next learning cycle is critical to setting up the next task.

Reflection can come in many forms, such as through journal postings, exit tickets, or reflection discussions. Give students time to clearly note how they felt throughout the learning phases, what they did that was successful or unsuccessful, and what they plan to do the next time around. As education philosopher John Dewey famously quoted, "We learn more from the reflection on the experience than we do from the experience itself."

Conclusion

It was over five years ago when Katie and Richard were working together at schools in Indiana and Ohio and they had this epiphany of the deep connections between self-regulation and reading. Reading is a psychosociolinguistic process and in order to be successful and independent readers, students must feel good about reading experiences (affective); be present in contexts where reading is encouraged (behaviors), modeled, and promoted; and provided with opportunities and strategies to develop deeper understanding (cognitive).

References and Resources

Bandura, A. (1977). Self-efficacy: Toward a unifying theory of behavioral change. *Psychological Review, 84*(2), 191.

Boekaerts, M., and Cascallar, E. (2006). How far have we moved toward the integration of theory and practice in self-regulation? *Educational Psychology Review, 18*(3), 199–210.

Boekaerts, M., and Corno, L. (2005). Self-regulation in the classroom: A perspective on assessment and intervention. *Applied Psychology, 54*(2), 199–231.

Cash, R. M. (2011). *Advancing differentiation: Thinking and learning for the 21st century.* Minneapolis: Free Spirit Publishing.

Cash, R. M. (2016a). *Self-regulation in the classroom: Helping students learn how to learn.* Minneapolis: Free Spirit Publishing.

Cash, R. M. (2016b). Self-regulation for learning. In K. S. McKnight, (Ed.), *Addressing the needs of all learners in the era of changing standards; Helping our most vulnerable students succeed through flexibility, innovation, and creativity* (pp. 31–52). Lanham, MD: Rowman & Littlefield.

Cohen, G. L., Garcia, J., Apfel, N., and Master, A. (2006). Reducing the racial achievement gap: A social-psychological intervention. *Science, 313*(5791), 1307–1310.

Conlon, E. G., Zimmer-Gembeck, M. J., Creed, P. A., and Tucker, M. (2006). Family history, self-perceptions, attitudes and cognitive abilities are associated with early adolescent reading skills. *Journal of Research in Reading, 29*(1), 11–32.

Connor, C. M., Ponitz, C. C., Phillips, B. M., Travis, Q. M., Glasney, S., and Morrison, F. J. (2010). First graders' literacy and self-regulation gains: The effect of individualizing student instruction. *Journal of School Psychology, 48*(5), 433–455.

Damasio, A. R. (1995). Review: Toward a neurobiology of emotion and feeling: Operational concepts and hypotheses. *The Neuroscientist, 1*(1), 19–25.

de Sousa, R. (2014, Spring). "Emotion." In the *Stanford Encyclopedia of Philosophy*, Edward N. Zalta (Ed.). Retrieved from http://plato.stanford.edu/archives/spr2014/entries/emotion/.

Dweck, C. (2006). *Mindset: The new psychology of success.* New York: Random House.

Eccles, J. S., and Wigfield, A. (2002). Motivational beliefs, values, and goals. *Annual Review of Psychology, 53*(1), 109–132.

Emmet, D. M. (1949). *The nature of metaphysical thinking.* London: MacMillan.

English, H. B., and English, A. C. (1958). *A comprehensive dictionary of psychological and psychoanalytical terms: A guide to usage.* [New York]: Longmans.

Lepper, M. R., Corpus, J. H., and Iyengar, S. S. (2005). Intrinsic and extrinsic motivational orientations in the classroom: Age differences and academic correlates. *Journal of Educational Psychology, 97*(2), 184.

Livingston, J. A. (1997). Metacognition: An overview. Retrieved from http://gse.buffalo.edu/fas/shuell/cep564/metacog.htm.

Locke, E. A., and Latham, G. P. (1990). *A theory of goal setting & task performance.* Englewood Cliffs, NJ: Prentice-Hall.

Moore, D. W., Bean, T. W., Birdyshaw, D., and Rycik, J. A. (1999). Adolescent literacy: A position statement. *Journal of Adolescent & Adult Literacy, 43*(1), 97–112.

J. Lee, W. Grigg, G. Dion – National Center for Education Statistics, 2007 – ERIC. *The Nation's Report Card [TM]: Mathematics 2007—National Assessment of Educational Progress at Grades 4 and 8.* NCES 2007-494.

J Lee, W Grigg, G Dion–National Center for Education Statistics, 2007–ERIC

Paris, S. G., and Paris, A. H. (2001). Classroom applications of research on self-regulated learning. *Educational Psychologist, 36*(2), 89–101.

Schunk, D., and Zimmerman, B. J. (Eds.). (2012). *Motivation and self-regulated learning: Theory, research and application.* New York: Routledge.

Smith, F. (2012). *Understanding reading: A psycholinguistic analysis of reading and learning to read.* New York: Routledge.

Sullivan, B. (2013, May 18). Students can't resist distraction for two minutes . . . and neither can you. *NBC News.*

Tough, P. (2013). *How children succeed: Grit, curiosity, and the hidden power of character.* London: Random House.

Vygotsky, L., M. Cole. (1987). Zone of proximal development. *Mind in Society: The Development of Higher Psychological Processes*, 52–91. Cambridge, MA: Harvard University Press.

Wiggins, G. (2012, September). Feedback for learning. *Educational Leadership, 70*(1), 10–16.

Zimmerman, B. J., Bonner, S., and Kovach, R. (1996). *Developing self-regulated learners: Beyond achievement to self-efficacy.* Washington, DC: American Psychological Association.

Zimmerman, B. J., and Kitsantas, A. (1999). Acquiring writing revision skills: Shifting from process to outcome self-regulatory goals. *Journal of Educational Psychology, 91, 1–10.*

Zimmerman, B. J., and Kitsantas, A. (2005). The hidden dimension of personal competence: Self-regulated learning and practice. In A. J. Elliot and C. S. Dweck (Eds.), *Handbook of Competence and Motivation* (pp. 509–526). New York: Guilford Press.

Zimmerman, B. J., and Schunk, D. H. (2001). Reflections on theories of self-regulated learning and academic achievement. In B. J. Zimmerman and D. H. Schunk (Eds.), *Self-regulated learning and academic achievement: Theoretical perspectives* (2nd ed., pp. 289–300). Mahwah, NJ: Lawrence Erlbaum.

Zimmerman, B. J., and Schunk, D. H. (Eds.). (2008). Motivation: An essential dimension of self-regulated learning. *Motivation and self-regulated learning: Theory, research, and applications* (pp. 1–30). New York: Lawrence Erlbaum.

Conclusion

The following email is from the eighth grade boy Bryce, who asked Lisa, "What makes you think you can teach me to read," to his high school guidance counselor (also named Lisa):

> Hello, Lisa, it's been awhile sense my last email and a lot happened, but I found a way to get it all together. I ended up only going to Viterbo just for that one semester, then took the spring off. Decided I wanted to give Iowa central another chance and went back, I wasn't eligible to run in the fall but I put in a lot of studying and hard work now I am running, not only I am running but I am getting a running scholarship and signing with another college to get my 4 year degree in criminal justice and may minor in psychology. This upcoming may I will be getting my AA in criminal just very excited, and I just thought I give you an up date and didn't want you to think I forgot about one of the people who helped me the most in high school, I am very grateful!!! Hope you pass the good news to Pam for me as well to another teaches that may ask about me.

What If We Would Have Given Up on Bryce?

Students in middle school and high school who struggle with reading can sometimes be ignored when it comes to intervention. They have somehow managed to get to where they are in school, but their skills are weak. As the rigor increases in their classes, their coping skills become less effective and even if they have managed to stay motivated, there is a lot less reward for their efforts. The achievement gap becomes wider and more difficult to close during the adolescent years.

When students are in elementary school, they are instructed by a teacher who has expertise in teaching the fundamentals of reading. At the middle and high school levels that stops and the timing could not be worse. The common belief is that now that students have learned to read, we can expect them to read to learn. The literacy demands increase exponentially, yet typically, schools do not teach adolescents how to successfully read the increasingly difficult materials they encounter throughout their day. Reading instruction needs to continue into middle school and high school, most especially for the students reading below grade level. For whatever reason, they didn't develop strong skills in elementary school, so now it is our responsibility to continue explicit reading instruction in middle and high school.

As Martha Hougen clarified in *Evidence-Based Reading Instruction for Adolescents Grades 6–12*, reports indicate that "there are an estimated six to eight million adolescents who struggle with reading in secondary schools" (Hougen, 2014). Some students with reading disabilities have been in special education or reading intervention classes since grade school. Some students' reading deficits only became apparent as the increasingly demanding reading tasks of middle school and high school finally exposed them as struggling readers. We can't ignore them.

"Secondary students with reading difficulties commonly have difficulties with decoding and fluency, which results in poor comprehension" (Hougen, 2014). "Difficulty mastering the basic skills of reading contribute to the low levels of comprehension, and adolescent students with reading disabilities typically require interventions that address word-level decoding and fluency development as well as comprehension" (Hougen, 2014).

As we mentioned in the introduction, the vast majority of middle and high school teachers did not have much, if any, secondary reading instruction or secondary reading intervention courses in college. Yet we are expected to have *all* of our students ready for college or career. An added layer of complexity for secondary teachers is that struggling readers are often embarrassed about their history of failure with respect to reading. They might try to conceal their shame with bad behavior, little motivation, or working hard to stay under the teachers' radar. Meanwhile—we have other students in our room counting on us to teach them content. It's a challenge, but there is something we can do to support these students. We can think of secondary students' reading requirements to include three components: word recognition and vocabulary (decoding), fluency (the bridge), and comprehension (understanding the content).

WORD RECOGNITION AND VOCABULARY (DECODING)

Core teachers can use explicit instruction in word recognition and vocabulary (decoding). Most students have mastered the letter-sound relationship, but for those who haven't, we have provided some strategies and activities in chapter 1. Core teachers can assist their students with word analysis by breaking down their content words and drawing attention to suffixes, prefixes, and root words. We have provided ideas and samples for that in chapter 1 as well. "Struggling adolescent readers may be able to read single-syllable words but must be taught strategies to decode multisyllabic words common in complex texts" (Hougen, 2014). Content area teachers can use the CLOVER model from chapter 2 to help their students learn to read and break apart unfamiliar words by syllable. Chapter 3 includes many ideas to help students "develop their understanding and knowledge of academic and domain-specific language."

FLUENCY (THE BRIDGE)

"Fluency is a significant variable in secondary students' reading and overall academic development" (Chard, 2012; Rasinski, Reutzel, Chard, and Thompson, 2011; Rasinski, Rikli, and Johnston, 2009). Chapter 4 has many effective practices to help students improve their fluency—thus building a strong bridge to comprehension.

COMPREHENSION (UNDERSTANDING THE CONTENT)

"Direct and explicit teaching of comprehension strategies is recommended for all students and is essential for students who struggle and those with disabilities" (Hougen, 2014). The tips, suggestions, and samples in chapter 5 are a good foundation for teaching comprehension strategies.

Additional comprehension assistance comes in the form of writing about reading and the value of reading aloud to secondary students—chapters 6 and 7. Chapter 8 teaches you to give and use the information from a running record to diagnose the exact reading difficulty so you can prescribe the solution. Finally, we close with a chapter on self-regulation, chapter 9. We can conduct a brilliant lesson that is the key to reading success, but if our students aren't motivated to be engaged, we haven't taught them a thing.

Reading involves a complex combination of word analysis and comprehension strategies. Struggling adolescent readers deserve the instruction that allows them to meet the rigorous challenges they face in school and eventually allows them to meet the increasing demands for literacy in the workforce. It is our responsibility.

References

Biancarosa, G., and Snow, C. E. (2004). *Reading next: A vision for action and research in middle and high school literacy: A report to Carnegie Corporation of New York.* Washington, DC: Alliance for Excellent Education.

Chard, D. J. Pikulski, J. J., and McDonagh, S. (2012). Fluency: The link between decoding and comprehension for struggling readers. In T. Rasinski, C. Blachoqicz, and K. Lems (Eds.), *Fluency Instruction: Research-Based Best Practices* (pp. 90–113). New York: Guilford.

Hougen, M. (2014). *Evidence-based reading instruction for adolescents, grades 6–12* (Document No. IC-13). Retrieved from University of Florida, Collaboration for Effective Educator, Development, Accountability, and Reform Center website: http://ceedar.education.ufl.edu/tools/innovation-configurations/.

Joftus, S., and Maddox-Dolan, B. (2003). *Left out and left behind: NCLB and the American high school. Every child a graduate.* Washington, DC: Alliance for Excellent Education.

Rasinski et al. (2005). *Is Reading Fluency a Key for Successful High School Reading?*

Rasinski, T. V. Reutzel, D. R., Chard, D., and Linan-Thompson, S. (2011). Reading fluency. In M. L. Kamil, P. D. Pearson, B. Moje, and P. Afflerbach (Eds.), *Handbook of Reading Research* (Vol. IV, pp. 286).

Scammacca, N., Roberts, G., Vaughn, S., and Stuebing, K. (2013). A meta-analysis of interventions for struggling readers in grades 4–12: 1980–2011. *Journal of Learning Disabilities.* Advance online publication. doi:10.1177/0022219413504995.

Vaughn, S., Denton, C., and Fletcher, J. (2010). Why intensive interventions are necessary for students with severe reading difficulties. *Psychology in the Schools, 47*(5), 432–444. doi:10.1002/pits.20481.

Index

About the Authors

Lisa Hollihan Allen, MSE, is a teacher, literacy coach, and author. She began her education career as a middle school language arts and literature teacher. She currently is a K–12 reading specialist for the West De Pere School District in Wisconsin where she works with students in grades 6–12 as a literacy interventionist. She serves as an adjunct instructor at St. Norbert College where she teaches the course Language Analysis and Applied Linguistics. Her role in education expanded when she worked as a literacy leader and literacy team facilitator for Wisconsin CESA 7 (Cooperative Educational Service Agency) extending educational opportunities to all corners of the state and across the nation. Lisa was a state finalist for the Kohl Teacher Fellowship.

Katherine McKnight, PhD, currently serves as a Distinguished Professor of Research at National Louis University. She travels worldwide as a professional development consultant and is a speaker in the fields of elementary and adolescent literacy, inclusive classrooms, state standards, interdisciplinary literacy, and integrating technology in the twenty-first-century classroom. She is completely committed to the development, sharing, and promotion of strategies that develop student literacy. That's why she spends many days each year in classrooms, working with teachers to help students grow into productive, creative adults. Because Katie's work takes her into all kinds of schools (public, private, parochial; rural, urban, and suburban), she's able to complement her vast expertise with relevant classroom experience. Dr. McKnight regularly publishes in professional journals and is the author of many award-winning, professional books.